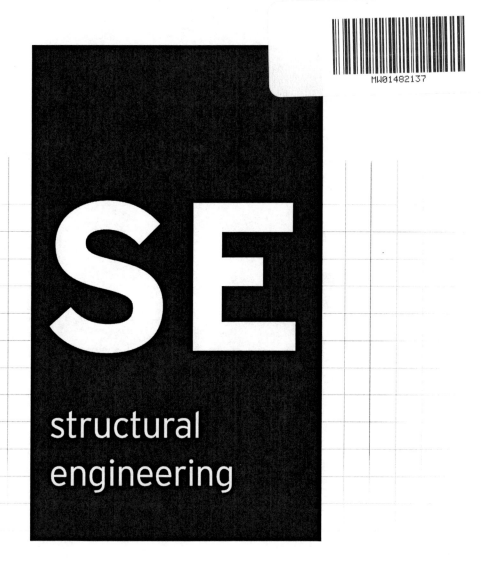

SE

structural
engineering

practice exam

NCEES
advancing licensure for
engineers and surveyors

978-1-932613-69-8

ISBN 978-1-932613-69-8

Printed in the United States of America
October 2014 First Printing

CONTENTS

About NCEES

The National Council of Examiners for Engineering and Surveying (NCEES) is a nonprofit organization made up of engineering and surveying licensing boards from all U.S. states and territories. Since its founding in 1920, NCEES has been committed to advancing licensure for engineers and surveyors in order to protect the health, safety, and welfare of the American public.

NCEES helps its member licensing boards carry out their duties to regulate the professions of engineering and surveying. It develops best-practice models for state licensure laws and regulations and promotes uniformity among the states. It develops and administers the exams used for engineering and surveying licensure throughout the country. It also provides services to help licensed engineers and surveyors practice their professions in other U.S. states and territories.

Updates on exam content and procedures

Visit us at **ncees.org/exams** for updates on everything exam-related, including specifications, exam-day policies, scoring, and corrections to published exam preparation materials. This is also where you will register for the exam and find additional steps you should follow in your state to be approved for the exam.

Exam-day schedule

Be sure to arrive at the exam site on time. Late-arriving examinees will not be allowed into the exam room once the proctor has begun to read the exam script. The report time for the exam will be printed on your Exam Authorization. Normally, you will be given 1 hour between morning and afternoon sessions.

Admission to the exam site

To be admitted to the exam, you must bring two items: (1) your Exam Authorization and (2) a current, signed, government-issued identification.

Examinee Guide

The *NCEES Examinee Guide* is the official guide to policies and procedures for all NCEES exams. All examinees are required to read this document before starting the exam registration process. You can download it at ncees.org/exams. It is your responsibility to make sure that you have the current version.

NCEES exams are administered in either a computer-based format or a pencil-and-paper format. Each method of administration has specific rules. This guide describes the rules for each exam format. Refer to the appropriate section for your exam.

Scoring and reporting

NCEES typically releases exam results to its member licensing boards 8–10 weeks after the exam. Depending on your state, you will be notified of your exam result online through your MyNCEES account or via postal mail from your state licensing board. Detailed information on the scoring process can be found at ncees.org/exams.

Staying connected

To keep up to date with NCEES announcements, events, and activities, connect with us on your preferred social media network.

Structural exam format

The 16-hour Structural exam is a breadth and depth exam offered in two components on successive days. The 8-hour Vertical Forces (Gravity/Other) and Incidental Lateral component is offered only on Friday. It focuses on gravity loads and includes minor lateral loads such as earth pressures. The 8-hour Lateral Forces (Wind/Earthquake) component is offered only on Saturday and focuses on wind/earthquake loads.

Each component of the structural exam has a breadth (morning) module and a depth (afternoon) module.
- Breadth modules (AM session): These modules contain questions covering a comprehensive range of structural engineering topics. All questions are multiple-choice.

- Depth modules (PM session): In these modules examinees must choose either buildings or bridges problems. Examinees must work the same topic area on both components. That is, if buildings is the topic area chosen in the Vertical Forces component, then buildings must be the topic area chosen in the Lateral Forces component. All questions are constructed response (essay).

Examinees must take the breadth module of each component and one of the two depth modules in each component. To pass the structural exam, you must receive acceptable results on both components. The components may be taken and passed in different exam administrations.

Summary of Structural Exam Format		
	Friday—Vertical Forces	**Saturday—Lateral Forces**
AM Session (Breadth)	40 multiple-choice questions (101–140) See p. 7 for details and specifications.	40 multiple-choice questions (101–140) See p. 127 for details and specifications.
PM Session (Depth)	Choose EITHER: Buildings (601–604) or Bridges (701–703) See p. 11 for details and specifications.	Choose EITHER: Buildings (801–804) or Bridges (901–903) See p. 131 for details and specifications.

NCEES will send a results notice to your licensing board each administration that you take a component. The notice will show the history of your performance on each component attempted. The results for each component will be listed as *acceptable* or *unacceptable*. After you have received an acceptable result on both components within a 5-year period, NCEES will notify your board that you have passed the Structural exam.

STRUCTURAL ENGINEERING Design Standards[1]

These standards apply to the Vertical and Lateral components of the Structural Engineering exam.
Changes to design standards are posted on ncees.org/exams.

Effective Beginning with the April 2015 Examinations

ABBREVIATION	DESIGN STANDARD TITLE
AASHTO	*AASHTO LRFD Bridge Design Specifications,* 6th edition, 2012, American Association of State Highway & Transportation Officials, Washington, DC.
IBC	*International Building Code,* 2012 edition (without supplements), International Code Council, Falls Church, VA.
ASCE 7	*Minimum Design Loads for Buildings and Other Structures,* 2010, American Society of Civil Engineers, Reston, VA.
ACI 318	*Building Code Requirements for Structural Concrete,* 2011, American Concrete Institute, Farmington Hills, MI.
AISC	*Steel Construction Manual,* 14th edition, American Institute of Steel Construction, Inc., Chicago, IL.
AISC	*Seismic Design Manual,* 2nd edition, American Institute of Steel Construction, Inc., Chicago, IL.
AISI	*North American Specification for the Design of Cold-Formed Steel Structural Members,* 2007 edition with Supplement No. 2 (2010), American Iron and Steel Institute, Washington, DC.
NDS	*National Design Specification for Wood Construction ASD/LRFD,* 2012 edition & *National Design Specification Supplement, Design Values for Wood Construction,* 2012 edition, American Forest & Paper Association, Washington, DC.
NDS	*Special Design Provisions for Wind and Seismic with Commentary,* 2008 edition, American Forest & Paper Association, Washington, DC.
PCI	*PCI Design Handbook: Precast and Prestressed Concrete,* 7th edition, 2010, Precast/Prestressed Concrete Institute, Chicago, IL.
TMS 402/602	*Building Code Requirements and Specifications for Masonry Structures* (and related commentaries), 2011; The Masonry Society, Boulder, CO; American Concrete Institute, Detroit, MI; and Structural Engineering Institute of the American Society of Civil Engineers, Reston, VA.

Notes
1. Solutions to exam questions that reference a standard of practice are scored based on this list. Solutions based on other editions or standards will not receive credit. All questions use the US Customary System (USCS) of units.

VERTICAL FORCES

VERTICAL FORCES EXAM SPECIFICATIONS

Vertical Forces (Gravity/Other) and Incidental Lateral Component of the Structural BREADTH Exam Specifications

Effective Beginning with the April 2011 Examinations

- The 4-hour **Vertical Forces (Gravity/Other) and Incidental Lateral** breadth examination is offered on Friday morning and focuses on gravity loads. It contains 40 multiple-choice questions.

- The exam uses the US Customary System (USCS) of units.

- The exam is developed with questions that will require a variety of approaches and methodologies, including design, analysis, and application.

- The knowledge areas specified as examples of kinds of knowledge are not exclusive or exhaustive categories.

- Score results are combined with depth exam results for final score of this component.

	Approximate Number of Questions
I. Analysis of Structures	**12**
A. Loads	4
B. Methods	8

I. Analysis of Structures — **12**

A. Loads — 4
1. Dead
2. Live
3. Snow, including drifting
4. Moving (e.g., vehicular, pedestrian, crane)
5. Thermal
6. Shrinkage and creep
7. Impact (e.g., vehicular, crane, and elevator)
8. Settlement
9. Ponding
10. Fluid
11. Ice
12. Static earth pressure
13. Hydrostatic
14. Hydraulics (e.g., stream flow, wave action, scour, flood)

B. Methods — 8
1. Statics (e.g., determinate, location of forces and moments, free-body diagrams)
2. Shear and moment diagrams
3. Code coefficients and tables
4. Computer-generated structural analysis techniques (e.g., modeling, interpreting, and verifying results)
5. Simplified analysis methods (e.g., influence lines, portal frame method/cantilever method)
6. Indeterminate analysis methods (e.g., deflection compatibility)

II. Design and Details of Structures — **26**

   A. General Structural Considerations — 3
     1. Material properties and standards
     2. Load combinations
     3. Serviceability requirements
       (a) Deflection
       (b) Camber
       (c) Vibration
     4. Fatigue (for AASHTO concrete and steel)
     5. Bearings
     6. Expansion joints
     7. Corrosion

   B. Structural Systems Integration — 1
     1. Specifications, quality controls and coordination with other disciplines
     2. Constructability
     3. Construction sequencing
     4. Strengthening existing systems: reinforcing methods

   C. Structural Steel — 5
     1. Tension members
     2. Columns and compression members
     3. Base plates
     4. Beams
     5. Plate girders—straight
     6. Plate girders—curved
     7. Trusses
     8. Beam-columns
     9. Connections—welded
     10. Connections—bolted
     11. Moment connections
     12. Weld design
     13. Composite steel design
     14. Relief angle (e.g., masonry support angle, facade support angle)
     15. Bridge piers
     16. Bridge cross-frame diaphragms

   D. Light Gage/Cold-Formed Steel — 1
     1. Framing
     2. Connections
     3. Web crippling

   E. Concrete — 5
     1. Flexural members (e.g., beams, joists, bridge decks, and slabs)
     2. Design for shear
     3. Columns and compression members
     4. Two-way slab systems
     5. Pre-tensioned concrete
     6. Post-tensioned concrete
     7. Attachment of elements and anchorage to concrete (e.g., inserts, attachment plates, dowels)

8. Bridge piers
9. Crack control
10. Composite design
11. Slab-on-grade

F. Wood   4
   1. Sawn beams
   2. Glue-laminated beams
   3. Engineered lumber
   4. Columns
   5. Bearing walls
   6. Trusses
   7. Bolted, nailed, and screwed connections

G. Masonry   3
   1. Flexural members
   2. Compression members
   3. Bearing walls
   4. Detailing (e.g., crack control, deflection, masonry openings)

H. Foundations and Retaining Structures   4
   1. Use of design pressure coefficients (e.g., active, passive, at rest, bearing, coefficient of friction, cohesion)
   2. Selection of foundation systems (e.g., based on geotechnical information, boring logs, settlement, and groundwater table)
   3. Overturning, sliding and bearing
   4. Combined footings/mat foundations
   5. Piles (concrete, steel, timber)
   6. Drilled shafts/drilled piers/caissons
   7. Gravity walls
   8. Anchored walls
   9. Cantilever walls
   10. Basement walls for buildings
   11. Effect of adjacent loads
   12. Use of modulus of sub-grade reaction

III. Construction Administration   **2**
  A. Procedures for Mitigating Nonconforming Work
  B. Inspection Methods

Vertical Forces (Gravity/Other) and Incidental Lateral Component of the Structural DEPTH Exam Specifications

Effective Beginning with the April 2011 Examination

The 4-hour **Vertical Forces (Gravity/Other) and Incidental Lateral** depth examination is offered on Friday afternoon. The depth modules of the Structural Engineering exam focus on a single area of practice in structural engineering. Examinees must choose either the **BUILDINGS** or the **BRIDGES** module. Examinees must work the same module on both components. That is, if bridges is the module chosen in the Vertical Forces component, then bridges must be the module chosen in the Lateral Forces component. All questions are constructed response (essay).

The exam uses the US Customary System (USCS) of units.

BUILDINGS

The **Vertical Forces (Gravity/Other) and Incidental Lateral** Structural Engineering depth exam in **BUILDINGS** covers loads, lateral earth pressures, analysis methods, general structural considerations (element design), structural systems integration (connections), and foundations and retaining structures. This 4-hour module contains one problem from each of the following areas:

- Steel structure
- Concrete structure
- Wood structure
- Masonry structure

All problems are equally weighted. At least one problem includes a multistory building, and at least one problem includes a foundation.

BRIDGES

The **Vertical Forces (Gravity/Other) and Incidental Lateral** Structural Engineering depth exam in **BRIDGES** covers gravity loads, superstructures, substructures, and lateral loads other than wind and seismic and may test pedestrian bridge and/or vehicular bridge knowledge. This 4-hour module contains three problems, one from each of the following areas:

- Concrete superstructure (25% of your score)
- Other elements of bridges (e.g., culverts, abutments, retaining walls) (25% of your score)
- Steel superstructure (50% of your score)

101. The figure shows an elevation view of a concrete highway bridge.

Design Code:
   AASHTO LRFD Bridge Design Specifications, 6th edition, 2012.

Design Data:
   Concrete modulus of elasticity $E_c = 3,605$ ksi
   Column moment of inertia $636,000$ in^4
   Coefficient of thermal expansion 6×10^{-6} in./in./°F
   Concrete shrinkage after 28 days $\varepsilon_{sh} = 0.0002$ in./in.

Assumptions:
   Columns are fixed at top of footing.
   Superstructure is pinned at the top of the columns.
   Bearings at the abutments are frictionless.
   Columns are very flexible compared to superstructure.

The unfactored horizontal load (kips) at the top of each column due to shrinkage after 28 days and a temperature fall of 40°F is most nearly:

(A)   14
(B)   70
(C)   159
(D)   263

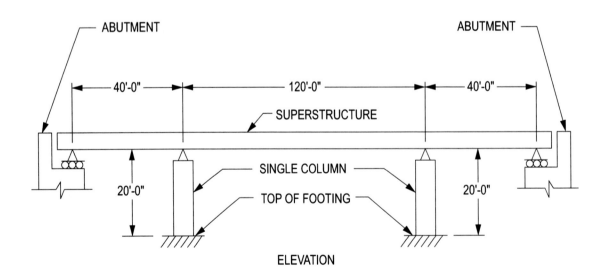

ELEVATION

102. A single-span concrete slab bridge is shown in the figure.

Design Code:
    AASHTO LRFD Bridge Design Specifications, 6th edition, 2012.

Design Data:
Live load	HL-93
Unfactored design truck moment per traffic lane	360 ft-kips

Assumption:
    Main flexural reinforcement is parallel to traffic.

The maximum factored design vehicular live load moment (ft-kips) for a Strength I limit state per traffic lane, including impact, is most nearly:

(A)   630
(B)   838
(C)   1,010
(D)   1,065

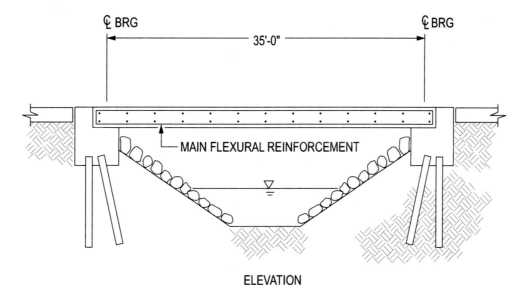

ELEVATION

103. The figure shows an essential facility that is located in a sheltered area.

Design Codes:
 IBC: *International Building Code,* 2012 edition (without supplements).
 ASCE 7: *Minimum Design Loads for Buildings and Other Structures,* 2010.

Design Data:
 Ground snow load $p_g = 30$ psf

The drift height, h_d (ft), shown on the figure is most nearly:

(A) 1.7
(B) 2.5
(C) 3.5
(D) 5.0

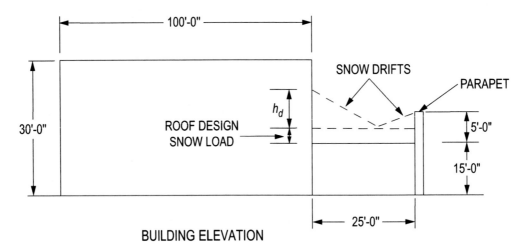

BUILDING ELEVATION

104. A crane rail supports a 5-kip vertical wheel load from a cab-operated bridge crane.

Design Code:
ASCE 7: *Minimum Design Loads for Buildings and Other Structures,* 2010.

The service vertical wheel load (kips), including impact, and the service longitudinal traction load (kips) on the crane rail are most nearly:

	Vertical Load	**Longitudinal Load**
(A)	4.00	1.00
(B)	5.00	5.00
(C)	6.25	0.25
(D)	6.25	0.50

105. A tied roof rafter is shown in the figure.

Assumptions:
All required factors have been applied to the given load.
The given load includes all imposed loads.

The moment (ft-lb) at Point D in Member B-C is most nearly:

(A) 219
(B) 1,750
(C) 2,625
(D) 3,500

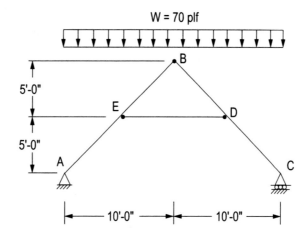

106. A highway bridge consists of a concrete deck slab supported on steel girders.

Design Code:
AASHTO LRFD Bridge Design Specifications, 6th edition, 2012.

Design Data:
Live load   HL-93

Assumptions:
The effective span length is 9'-6".
The deck slab is supported on seven girders.

The negative live load moment (ft-kips) including impact in an interior span of the deck slab per foot width of slab at the centerline of the girder is most nearly:

(A)   6.59
(B)   7.15
(C)   8.76
(D)   9.51

107. A plate that is simply supported along its four edges is shown in the figure.

Assumptions:
    Use either triangle or quad or combinations of plate elements in the computer model.
    Plate elements do not have midside nodes.

The correct mesh to model the plate for computer analysis is most nearly:

(A)

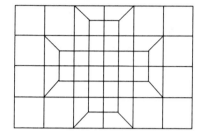

(B)

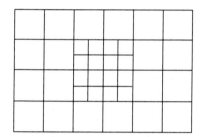

(C)

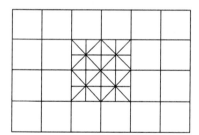

(D)

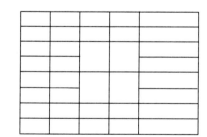

108. The eccentrically loaded footing A is connected to the concentrically loaded footing B by a strap beam as shown in the figure.

Assumptions:
   The loads and reactions shown have been factored.
   Disregard sign convention.

The factored shears (kips) and moments (ft-kips) at the strap beam ends are most nearly:

	V_{ab}	M_{ab}	V_{ba}	M_{ba}
(A)	12.0	38.0	19.0	38.0
(B)	13.0	25.0	20.0	40.0
(C)	1.5	30.0	0.3	0.6
(D)	1.3	12.4	0.3	0.6

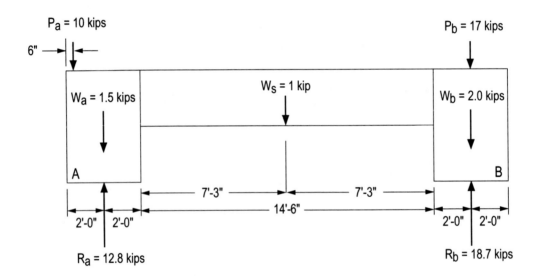

109. The beam shown is subjected to a uniform load and a moving concentrated load.

Design Data:
    Uniform live load   1 klf
    Concentrated live load   10 kips

Assumption:
    The uniform live load may extend the entire length of the beam from A to C.

The maximum live load shear (kips) on the right of Support B is most nearly:

(A)   32
(B)   36
(C)   40
(D)   46

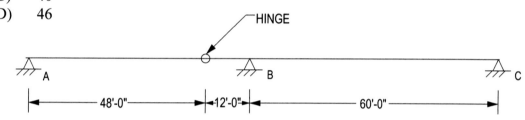

110. The figure shows a line diagram for a continuous beam that is supported as shown. The distribution factors at Joint B for Spans BA and BC are most nearly:

	BA	**BC**
(A)	0.33	0.67
(B)	0.43	0.57
(C)	0.5	0.5
(D)	0.67	0.33

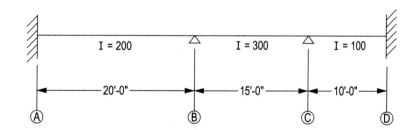

111. The figure shows the loads acting on a beam.

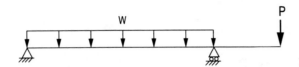

The shear diagram is most nearly:

(A)

(B)

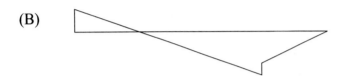

(C)

(D)

112. The figure shows a line diagram of a beam. The influence line for the moment at Support A is most nearly:

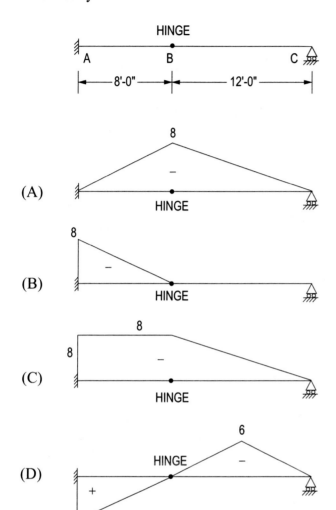

113. The figures show an elevation view and a plan view of a bearing for a highway bridge girder.

Design Code:
AASHTO LRFD Bridge Design Specifications, 6th edition, 2012.

Design Data:
Abutment f'_c = 4 ksi at 28 days
Strength limit state reaction for the end of the girder   415 kips

Assumptions:
Assume uniform distribution of bearing pressure.
$A_2 = A_1$

The **minimum** width (in.) of bearing plate required is most nearly:

(A)   8
(B)   13
(C)   16
(D)   22

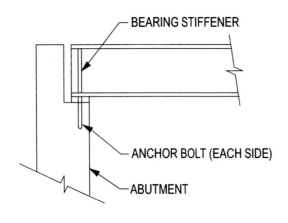

BEARING ELEVATION

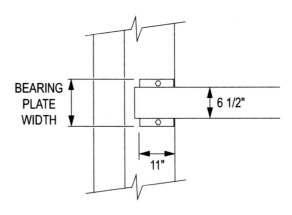

BEARING PLAN

114. When a concrete slab is placed on a hot, windy day, it is **not** permissible to:

(A) keep mix water cool and aggregate moist by shading and sprinkling

(B) add field water as needed to obtain the desired consistency and workability

(C) spray the concrete surfaces or protect them with wet burlap to retard hardening

(D) moisten the forms and the reinforcement before placing the concrete to minimize evaporation

115. A highway bridge consists of steel girders.

Design Code:
  AASHTO LRFD Bridge Design Specifications, 6th edition, 2012.

Design Data:

Total service dead load moment (DC)	1,200 ft-kips
Total service live load moment including dynamic load allowance	850 ft-kips
Total service dead load moment due to wearing surface (DW)	100 ft-kips

The design moment (ft-kips) using the Strength I loading combination with maximum load factors is most nearly:

(A) 2,912
(B) 3,138
(C) 3,438
(D) 3,684

116. You are working as a quality control representative for a contractor on a project. If you discover a potentially unsafe condition at the project site, the initial action you should take is to:

(A)   stop the construction of the project

(B)   report the condition to the contractor

(C)   report the condition to the owner

(D)   report the condition to OSHA

117. A built-up column section is shown.

Design Code:
    AISC: *Steel Construction Manual,* 14th edition.

Design Data:
    Steel   ASTM A 36, F_y = 36 ksi

Assumptions:
    K = 1.0
    The unbraced lengths in the X and Y directions are 10 ft.

The critical buckling stress F_{cr} (ksi) is most nearly:

(A)   22
(B)   26
(C)   35
(D)   48

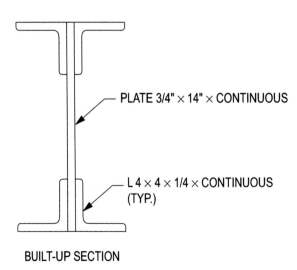

PLATE 3/4" × 14" × CONTINUOUS

L 4 × 4 × 1/4 × CONTINUOUS
(TYP.)

BUILT-UP SECTION

118. An elevation view of a bolted beam splice of a continuous beam bridge is shown in the figure.

Design Code:
    AASHTO LRFD Bridge Design Specifications, 6th edition, 2012.

Design Data:
    Unfactored moments at the splice location are:
        Dead load (DC)   25.8 ft-kips
        Live load plus dynamic load allowance (max)   492.7 ft-kips
    Structural steel yield strength   50 ksi

Assumptions:
    Beams are continuously braced and noncompact.
    Resistance factor, $\phi_f = 1.00$.
    Beams are noncomposite.
    Flexural resistance of member shall be based on elastic section properties.

Using Strength I combination, the required **minimum** factored flexural resistance (ft-kips) of the splice is most nearly:

(A)   895
(B)   1,372
(C)   1,498
(D)   2,100

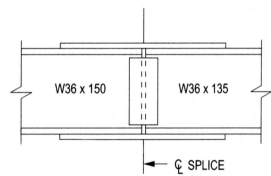

119. A simply supported composite W24 × 76 girder has a span length of 60 ft. The girder is not shored.

Design Code:
    AISC: *Steel Construction Manual,* 14th edition.

Design Data:
    Wet weight of concrete   600 plf
    Superimposed dead load   344 plf

The portion of the dead load moment (ft-kips) carried by the steel section is most nearly:

(A)   459
(B)   304
(C)   270
(D)   34

120. The figure shows a typical steel rigid frame for a warehouse.

Design Code:
   AISC: *Steel Construction Manual,* 14th edition.

Design Data:
   $F_y = 50.0$ ksi
   $K_x = 2.0$
   $K_y = 1.0$

For ASD option:
   $M_{rx} = 113$ ft-kips
   $M_n/\Omega = 173$ ft-kips

For LRFD option:
   $M_{ux} = 180$ ft-kips
   $\phi_b M_{nx} = 262$ ft-kips

Top of Column Conditions	
Load	Compressive Axial Force (kips)
Dead (D)	7.2
Roof Live (L_r)	12.6
Wind (W)	6.4

Assumptions:
   A W14 × 53 section has been selected for Column AB.
   ASD controlling load combination is $D + 0.75\,L_r + 0.45\,W$.
   LRFD controlling load combination is $1.2\,D + 1.6\,L_r + 0.5\,W$.

The ratio for the interaction of flexure and compression for Column AB is most nearly:

	ASD	**LRFD**
(A)	0.750	0.774
(B)	0.733	0.745
(C)	0.693	0.730
(D)	0.672	0.716

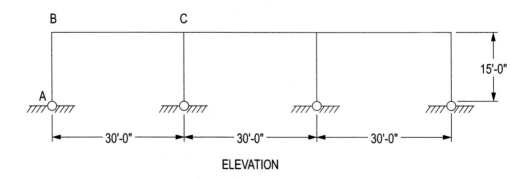

ELEVATION

28

121. The figure shows a column and base plate.

Design Code:
   AISC: *Steel Construction Manual,* 14th edition.

Design Data:
Base plate	F_y = 36 ksi
Column	F_y = 50 ksi
W14 × 53 column effective length	12 ft
Column axial load	150 kips (ASD) or 190 kips (LRFD)

Assumption:
   The base plate has full contact area to concrete support.

The minimum required thickness (in.) of the base plate is most nearly:

	ASD	**LRFD**
(A)	3/8	1/4
(B)	1/2	3/8
(C)	5/8	1/2
(D)	3/4	5/8

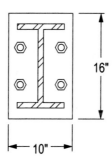

122. A cold-formed steel box header is constructed using two 800S200-33 sections as shown.

Design Code:

AISI: *North American Specification for the Design of Cold-Formed Steel Structural Members,* 2007 edition with Supplement No. 2 (2010).

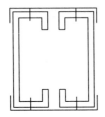

Design Data:

$F_y = 33$ ksi

| Section | Design Thickness | Gross | | | | | | | Effective | |
| | | Area | Weight | Ixx | Sxx | Rx | Iyy | Ry | Ixx | Sxx |
	(in.)	(in²)	(lb/ft)	(in⁴)	(in³)	(in.)	(in⁴)	(in.)	(in⁴)	(in³)
800S200-33	0.0346	0.448	1.52	4.096	1.024	3.023	0.227	0.712	4.096	0.812
800S200-43	0.0451	0.582	1.98	5.302	1.325	3.018	0.292	0.708	5.302	1.293
800S200-54	0.0566	0.726	2.47	6.573	1.643	3.009	0.357	0.701	6.573	1.643
800S200-68	0.0713	0.907	3.09	8.140	2.035	2.996	0.435	0.692	8.140	2.035
800S200-97	0.1017	1.271	4.32	11.203	2.801	2.969	0.576	0.673	11.203	2.801

Assumptions:

The header is fully braced. Lateral-torsional buckling need not be considered.

The track sections stiffen the flanges of the 800S200 sections.

The maximum allowable moment (ASD) or design moment (LRFD) (ft-lb) for the cold-formed steel box header is most nearly:

	ASD	**LRFD**
(A)	1,377	2,233
(B)	2,674	4,243
(C)	3,372	5,632
(D)	4,052	6,767

123. An interior prestressed concrete girder for a two-lane, simply supported highway bridge with a 76-ft span is to be designed. The figure shows a typical interior girder section with the preliminary arrangement of the prestressing strands.

Design Code:
 AASHTO LRFD Bridge Design Specifications, 6th edition, 2012.

Design Data:

Weight of girder	822 plf
Prestressing force at release	650 kips
Area of girder	789 in^2
Section moduli for the girder:	
Top fiber	8.089 in^3
Bottom fiber	10,543 in^3

The concrete stress distribution at midspan at release of prestress is most nearly:

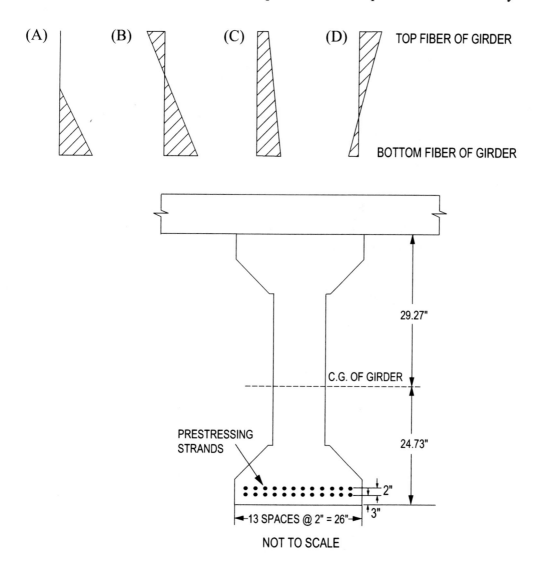

NOT TO SCALE

124. The figure shows a cast-in-place concrete slab and beam inside an office building.

Design Code:
ACI 318: *Building Code Requirements for Structural Concrete*, 2011.

Design Data:
Cast-in-place concrete $f'_c = 3,000$ psi

Assumption:
The slab and beam are adequate for all loading conditions.

The nominal maximum size of coarse aggregate (in.) that can be used in the concrete mix is most nearly:

(A)   1 1/8
(B)   1 1/2
(C)   1 2/3
(D)   2

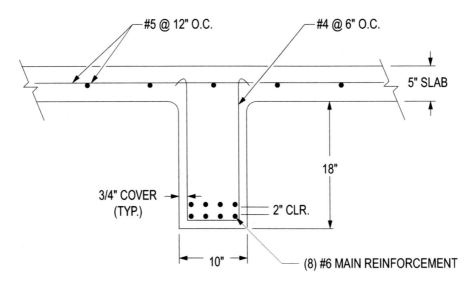

GO ON TO THE NEXT PAGE

125. An elevation and a section through a reinforced concrete bridge pier are shown in the figure.

Design Code:
  AASHTO LRFD Bridge Design Specifications, 6th edition, 2012.

Design Data:
  f'_c = 4 ksi
  f_y = 60 ksi

The effective shear depth d_v (in.) of the cantilever of the pier cap at the face of the wall is most nearly:

(A)   43.2
(B)   51.6
(C)   54.9
(D)   57.3

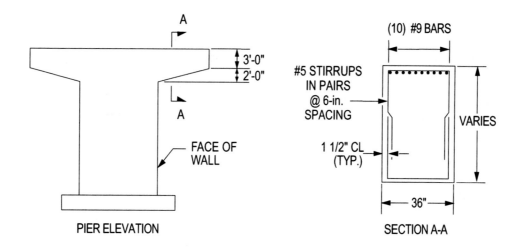

PIER ELEVATION   SECTION A-A

126. The figure shows a portion of a multistory, unbraced reinforced concrete frame.

Design Code:
   ACI 318: *Building Code Requirements for Structural Concrete*, 2011.

Design Data:
   $f'_c = 4,000$ psi

Assumptions:
   Section 10.10.4.1 of ACI 318-11 is applicable.

The effective length factor k of the 16-in. × 16-in column indicated on the figure is most nearly:

(A)   1.25
(B)   1.45
(C)   1.75
(D)   2.0

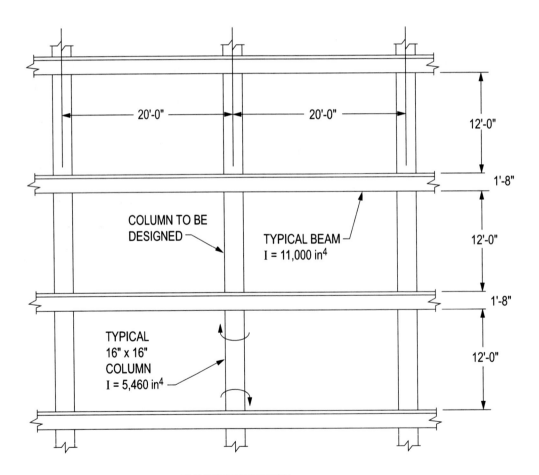

BUILDING ELEVATION

34   GO ON TO THE NEXT PAGE

127. A 16-in. × 16-in. reinforced concrete column bears on a concrete footing.

Design Code:
ACI 318: *Building Code Requirements for Structural Concrete*, 2011.

Design Data:
Normal weight concrete
Concrete strength $f'_c = 4,000$ psi
Yield stress of reinforcing steel $f_y = 60$ ksi

The minimum embedment length (in.) to develop a #11 compression bar is most nearly:

(A) 13
(B) 17
(C) 22
(D) 27

128. The figure shows a bolted connection.

Design Code:
NDS: *National Design Specification for Wood Construction ASD/LRFD*, 2012 edition & *National Design Specification Supplement, Design Values for Wood Construction*, 2012 edition.

Design Data:
All wood members Southern Pine
Bolt bearing yield strength $F_{yb} = 45$ ksi
Bolt diameter 5/8 in.

Assumptions:
Loading is perpendicular to the bolt and parallel with the grain.
Ignore reductions for end distance and/or edge distance.

The reference design value (lb) for the connection is most nearly:

(A) 1,000
(B) 1,250
(C) 1,870
(D) 3,250

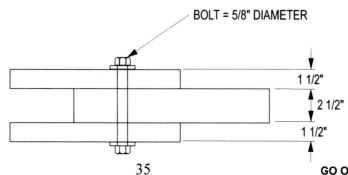

129. A roof dead load and snow load is supported by 2 × 10 Hem-Fir No. 2 rafters spaced at 24 in. o.c.

Design Code:

NDS: *National Design Specification for Wood Construction ASD/LRFD*, 2012 edition & *National Design Specification Supplement, Design Values for Wood Construction*, 2012 edition.

Assumptions:

Bending controls the design
$C_M = C_t = C_{fu} = C_i = 1.0$
$C_L = 0.986$
$\lambda = 0.8$

The adjusted design moment (in.-lb) of the roof rafters is most nearly:

	ASD	LRFD
(A)	17,000	26,000
(B)	18,000	27,000
(C)	26,000	39,000
(D)	36,000	54,000

130. The figure shows the elevation view of an existing glulam beam (GLB) that was designed to span between supports A and B. Because of an increase in the loading, a post was added at the midspan of the GLB as shown.

Design Code:
   NDS: *National Design Specification for Wood Construction ASD/LRFD*, 2012 edition & *National Design Specification Supplement, Design Values for Wood Construction*, 2012 edition.

Design Data:
   The combination symbol and species of the GLB are shown in the figure.

Assumptions:
   All adjustment factors are 1.0, except K_f, ϕ_b, and λ if LRFD method is used.
   $\lambda = 0.8$

The adjusted moment capacity M'_n (ft-kips) in the GLB at the post is most nearly:

	ASD	**LRFD**
(A)	16.0	27.6
(B)	11.6	20.0
(C)	9.6	16.7
(D)	8.0	13.8

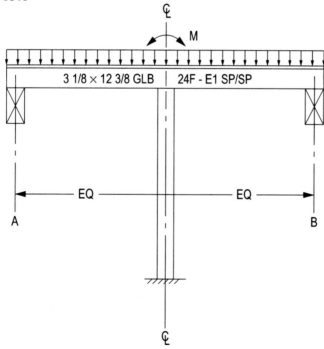

131. An 8 × 8 wood post supports a dead load and a live load.

Design Code:
  NDS: *National Design Specification for Wood Construction ASD/LRFD*, 2012 edition & *National Design Specification Supplement, Design Values for Wood Construction*, 2012 edition.

Design Data:
  Douglas-Fir Larch, Grade No. 1

Assumptions:
  $F_{cE} / F_c^* = 0.957$
  No lateral support is provided between supports.
  Column is pinned at the top and bottom.
  $C_D = C_M = C_t = C_F = C_i = 1.0$
  $\lambda = 0.8$
  Lumber is visually graded.

The adjusted compression design value (psi) parallel to grain is most nearly:

	ASD	**LRFD**
(A)	510	880
(B)	670	1,160
(C)	730	1,260
(D)	1,000	1,730

132. An anchor bolt in masonry is shown in the figure.

Design Codes:

TMS 402/602: *Building Code Requirements and Specifications for Masonry Structures* (and related commentaries), 2011.

Design Data:

$f'_m = 1,500$ psi
$f_y = 36,000$ psi

Assumptions:

Bent anchor bolt   5/8-in. diameter
Masonry solid grouted

The design tension T (lb) is most nearly:

	ASD	**LRFD**
(A)	2,300	3,800
(B)	3,800	6,100
(C)	6,700	10,000
(D)	11,200	17,900

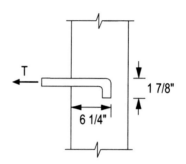

133. The figure shows an 8-in. reinforced concrete masonry wall.

Design Code:
TMS 402/602: *Building Code Requirements and Specifications for Masonry Structures* (and related commentaries), 2011.

Design Data:
Hollow concrete masonry units $f'_m = 1,500$ psi with Type S mortar.
Cells with reinforcement are grouted.
Steel reinforcement ASTM A615 Grade 60

Assumptions:
Seismic forces do not govern.
The wall is reinforced with #5 @ 48-in. o.c. vertically at the centerline of the wall and #5 @ 32-in. o.c. horizontally.

The design axial load (plf) for the masonry wall is most nearly:

	ASD	**LRFD**
(A)	14,200	32,400
(B)	25,500	59,400
(C)	39,300	91,500
(D)	107,300	249,900

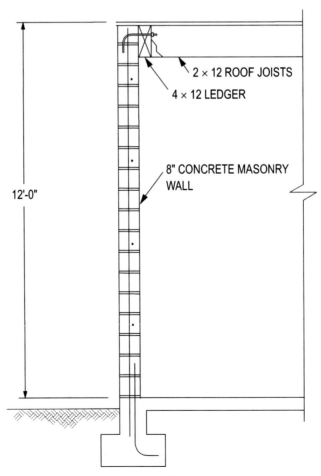

GO ON TO THE NEXT PAGE

134. The figure shows an 8-in. reinforced concrete masonry wall.

Design Code:

TMS 402/602: *Building Code Requirements and Specifications for Masonry Structures* (and related commentaries), 2011.

Design Data:

Hollow concrete masonry units $f'_m = 1,500$ psi with Type S mortar.
Cells with reinforcement are grouted.
Steel reinforcement ASTM A615 Grade 60

Assumptions:

Allowable stress design provisions apply.
The wall is reinforced with #5 @ 48-in. o.c. vertically at the centerline of the wall and #5 @ 32-in. o.c. horizontally.

The maximum allowable moment (ft-lb/ft) on the masonry wall based on the maximum allowable masonry flexural stress is most nearly:

(A)   665
(B)   1,070
(C)   1,465
(D)   2,335

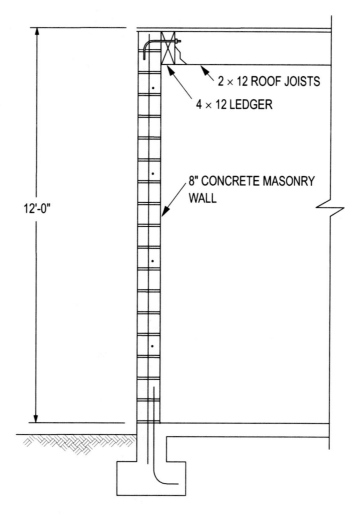

135. A rectangular pile cap for a single square column is supported by six piles as shown in the figure.

Design Data:
Unfactored loads at the bottom of the column are:
Axial vertical load, P   250 kips
Moment, M_{xx} 320 ft-kips
Moment, M_{yy} 225 ft-kips

Assumption:
Both moments occur at the same time.

The maximum unfactored axial load (kips) in a pile is most nearly:

(A)   34
(B)   48
(C)   76
(D)   83

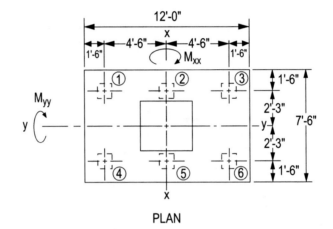

PLAN

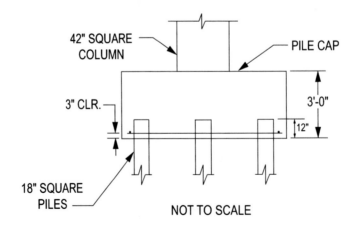

NOT TO SCALE

136. The plan and elevation views of a square footing supporting a column are shown in the figure.

Design Data:
  Net allowable soil bearing pressure   4,000 psf
  The service loads are as indicated.

Assumptions:
  Neglect the weight of the soil and the footing in the calculations.
  No net uplift under loads shown.

The minimum dimension B (ft) required for the footing is most nearly:

(A)   3.7
(B)   5.5
(C)   5.9
(D)   7.0

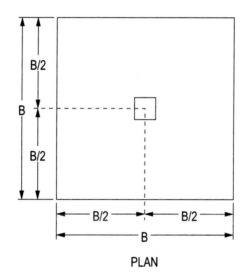

PLAN

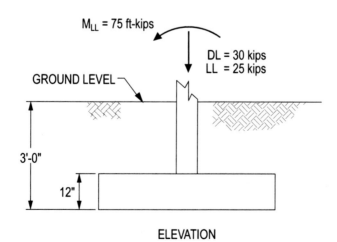

ELEVATION

43   **GO ON TO THE NEXT PAGE**

137. The reinforced concrete retaining wall section with the most efficient footing configuration and steel reinforcement is:

(A)

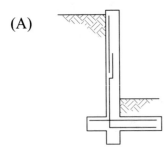

(B)

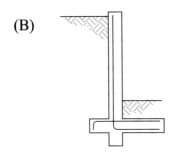

(C)

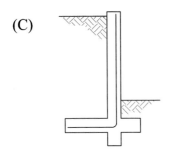

(D)

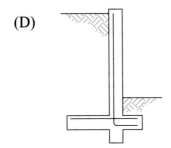

138. The eccentrically loaded footing A is connected to the concentrically loaded footing B by a strap beam as shown in the figure.

Design Data:
   The axial loads and weights shown have been factored.

The factored footing reactions, R_a and R_b, (kips) shown in the figure are most nearly:

	R_a	R_b
(A)	370	435
(B)	250	295
(C)	210	210
(D)	195	230

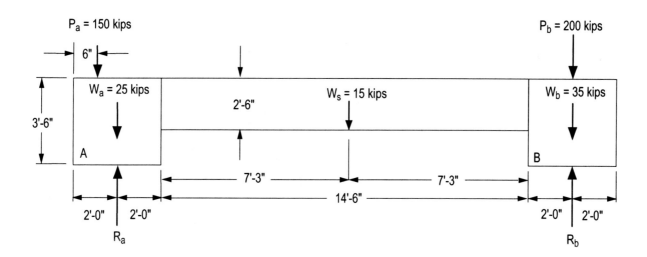

45 **GO ON TO THE NEXT PAGE**

139. A contractor has placed the incorrect steel beam section in the floor structure of a new building. The discovery of the error was made after the concrete-over-metal deck floor slab was placed. To resolve the issue, a continuous plate will be added to the underside of the flange of the beam, as shown in the figure, to increase its capacity.

Design Data:
Capacity of 3/16" fillet weld   2.78 kips/in.
Maximum design shear in the beam   40 kips

The minimum adequate welding pattern to connect the added continuous plate to the beam is most nearly:

(A)   1.5 in. at 12 in. on center each side of plate

(B)   2 in. at 12 in. on center each side of plate

(C)   3 in. at 12 in. on center each side of plate

(D)   continuous weld each side of plate

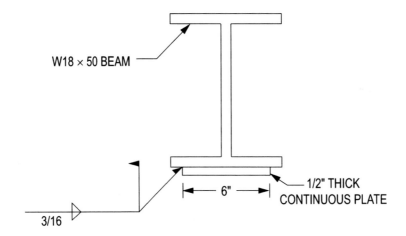

140. Which of the following is **not** required in the statement of special inspections?

(A) Type and extent of each test

(B) Identification of continuous or periodic special inspections for each type of special inspection

(C) Materials, systems, components, and work required to have special inspections

(D) Name and address of inspector performing work

This completes the morning session. Solutions begin on page 69.

VERTICAL FORCES PM BUILDINGS PRACTICE EXAM

601. The first floor of a three-story apartment building is partially buried as shown in **Figure 601A.**

Design Codes:
IBC: *International Building Code,* 2012 edition (without supplements).
ASCE 7: *Minimum Design Loads for Buildings and Other Structures,* 2010.
TMS 402/602: *Building Code Requirements and Specifications for Masonry Structures* (and Related Commentaries), 2011.
ACI 318: *Building Code Requirements for Structural Concrete,* 2011.

Design Data:
Masonry	f'_m = 2,000 psi
Grout	f'_c = 2,000 psi
Reinforcing	ASTM A615, Grade 60
Masonry weight (per surface area)	84 psf
Concrete	f'_c = 3,000 psi
Concrete density	150 pcf
Soil weight	110 pcf
Rankine coefficient of passive soil pressure	2.5
Rankine coefficient of active soil pressure	0.35
Allowable soil bearing pressure	3,000 psf
Coefficient of static friction (concrete on soil)	0.28

Assumptions:
Neglect wind and seismic loads.
No hydrostatic pressure on wall.
Wall is not backfilled until construction is complete.
Neglect slab on grade and soil over toe side of footing.

REQUIREMENTS:

On the actual exam, any sketches necessary for these requirements must be neatly drawn in your solution pamphlet.

(a) For the CMU wall design shown in **Figure 601A,** verify that the wall stem is adequate for vertical loads shown and provided soil information. Use IBC load combination equation 16-2 (LRFD) or 16-11 (ASD). Do not use load information given in **Figure 601B** for this requirement.

(b) For the footing shown in **Figure 601B,** show by calculation whether the footing size subjected to the loads indicated is or is not adequate for bearing and stability. Do not use vertical load data provided for **Requirement (a).**

(c) Neatly sketch the connection of the masonry wall to the concrete footing. Show the required dimensions of the embedment and anchorage of the steel reinforcement to the footing.

601. (Continued)

FIGURE 601A FOR **REQUIREMENT (a)** ONLY

CONCENTRIC LOAD (P) FROM ALL ELEMENTS

TOTAL DL = 980 plf
FLOOR LL = 640 plf
ROOF LL   = 160 plf

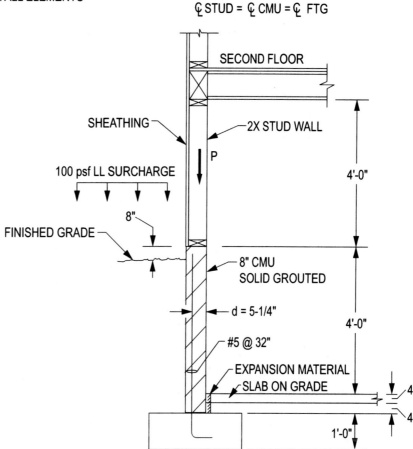

CL STUD = CL CMU = CL FTG

SECOND FLOOR

SHEATHING

2X STUD WALL

P

100 psf LL SURCHARGE

4'-0"

8"

FINISHED GRADE

8" CMU
SOLID GROUTED

d = 5-1/4"

4'-0"

#5 @ 32"

EXPANSION MATERIAL
SLAB ON GRADE

4"

4"

1'-0"

FIGURE 601A

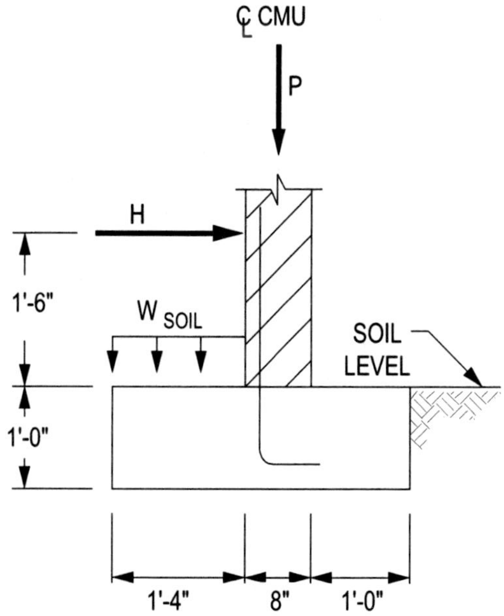

CL CMU

P

H

1'-6"

W SOIL

SOIL
LEVEL

1'-0"

1'-4"   8"   1'-0"

FIGURE 601B

FIGURE 601B FOR REQUIREMENT (b) ONLY

LOAD (P) AT CL OF CMU

TOTAL DL = 3,000 plf (NOT INCL. FTG. WT.)

TOTAL HORIZONTAL FORCE DUE TO
SOIL & SURCHARGE LOADS, H = 600 plf

VERTICAL SOIL LOAD ON HEEL, W_{SOIL} = 450 psf

602. An elevation of a two-story steel office building is shown in **Figure 602A.** The columns are continuous. The beams are pinned except for the two-story moment frame between Grids B and C.

Design Codes:
    IBC: *International Building Code,* 2012 edition (without supplements).
    AISC: *Steel Construction Manual*, 14th edition.

Design Data:

Steel beam and column	ASTM A992, F_y = 50 ksi
Steel plate	ASTM A36, F_y = 36 ksi, F_u = 58 ksi
Bolts, 3/4-in. diameter	A325-N
Service dead load on Member 10	850 plf, all-inclusive
Service floor live load on Member 10	1,250 plf, non-reducible
Weld rod	E70XX

Assumption:
    Neglect lateral loads and lateral criteria for this problem.

REQUIREMENTS:

On the actual exam, any sketches necessary for these requirements must be neatly drawn in your solution pamphlet.

(a)   Using the unit load output data shown in **Figure 602B,** determine the shears and moments in Member 10 and draw and label the shear and moment diagrams. Use IBC load combination Equation 16-2.

(b)   Design the beam-to-column connection for Member 10 at Joint 5 for the loads from **Requirement (a).** Use a bolted flange-plate fully rigid moment connection per **Figure 602C.**

(c)   Neatly sketch the connection including shear and flange plate sizes, welds, and bolts.

602. (Continued)

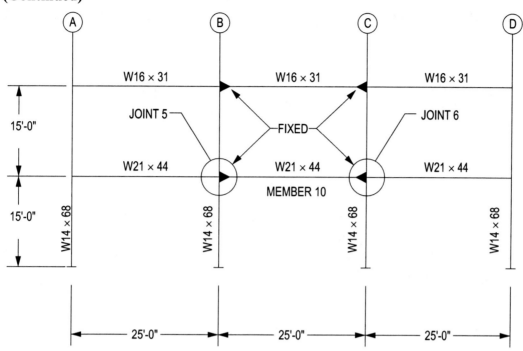

FIGURE 602A

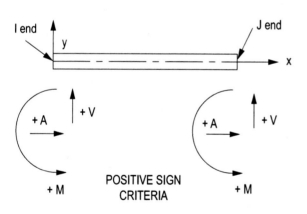

I end   J end
y
x

POSITIVE SIGN
CRITERIA

+ A   + V   + M (I end)
+ A   + V   + M (J end)

The following forces are from a uniform unit load of 1,000 plf:

Joint 5
A − 2.0 kips
V +12.5 kips
M + 44.0 ft-kips

Joint 6
A + 2.0 kips
V +12.5 kips
M − 44.0 ft-kips

FIGURE 602B

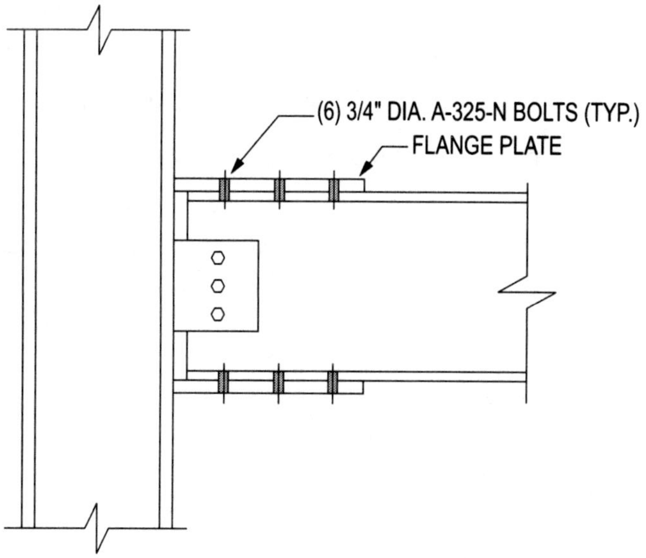

(6) 3/4" DIA. A-325-N BOLTS (TYP.)
FLANGE PLATE

FIGURE 602C

603. A three-story concrete building is constructed with ordinary concrete shear walls as shown in **Figure 603.** Beams and columns on Lines B, C, 2, and 3 do not resist any lateral loads. All gravity loads are supported by the concrete frame system.

Design Codes:
    IBC: *International Building Code,* 2012 edition (without supplements).
    ASCE 7: *Minimum Design Loads for Buildings and Other Structures,* 2010.
    ACI 318: *Building Code Requirements for Structural Concrete,* 2011.

Design Data:
Floor dead load	130 psf (including all building weights)
Floor live load	70 psf (reducible)
Concrete	$f_c' = 4{,}000$ psi at 28 days
Reinforcing	$f_y = 60{,}000$ psi
Concrete density	144 pcf

Beams are 18 in. wide and 24 in. deep.
Slab is 9 in. thick.

Assumptions:
    Neglect partition loads.

REQUIREMENTS:

On the actual exam, any sketches necessary for these requirements must be neatly drawn in your solution pamphlet.

(a)   Determine the factored shears and moments in a continuous floor beam on Grid Line C between Grids 3 and 4. Use ACI coefficients.

(b)   Sketch the shear and moment diagrams for the beam in **Requirement (a).**

(c)   Design the beam for the positive moment in the span and the negative moment and shear at Column 3.

(d)   Show all of the beam reinforcing required at Joint 1 in an elevation sketch. Include, but do not design, the column steel.

603. (Continued)

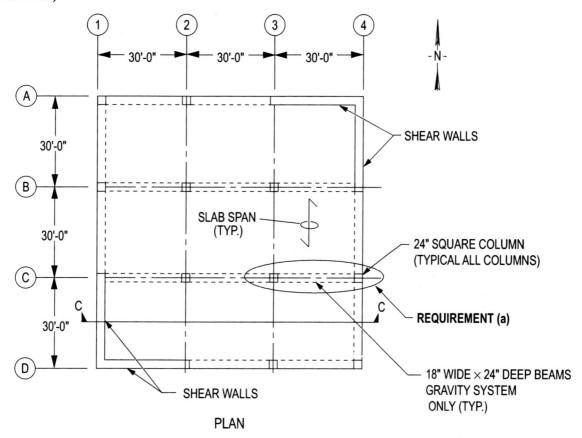

PLAN

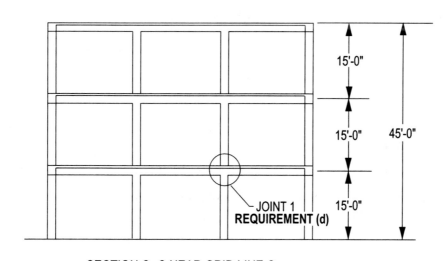

SECTION C–C NEAR GRID LINE C

FIGURE 603

604. An existing warehouse roof is framed with glulam girders and purlins at girder quarter points. In order to install new equipment that conflicts with portions of the existing roof framing, it is proposed to remove a portion of the existing roof framing per **Figure 604A,** convert the existing glulam girder into a truss, and install a new roof enclosure as shown in **Figure 604B.**

Design Codes:
> IBC: *International Building Code*, 2012 edition (without supplements).
> ASCE 7: *Minimum Design Loads for Buildings and Other Structures*, 2010.
> AISC: *Steel Construction Manual*, 14th edition.
> NDS: *National Design Specification for Wood Construction ASD/LRFD*, 2012 edition & *National Design Specification Supplement, Design Values for Wood Construction*, 2012 edition.

Design Data:
> Existing glulam girder 8 1/2" × 26 1/8" Southern Pine stress class 24F-1.7E
> New center post   8 × 8 Southern Pine No. 2
> New steel plate   ASTM A36
> New bolts   ASTM A307
> Existing condition loads per **Figure 604C** (after demolition and without new tension rods).
> New equipment load per **Figure 604D** (with new tension rods in place).
> Properties of existing glulam girder are given in **Table 604A.**

Assumptions:
> The existing glulam girder is not shored during construction and is laterally braced only at the purlins.
> Ignore wind and seismic loads.
> Neglect weight of the glulam girder, the steel rods, and all miscellaneous steel connection plates.
> Ignore all live loads. Only use loads indicated in **Figure 604C** and **Figure 604D.**

REQUIREMENTS:

(a) Determine the forces in each of the members of the new truss for the final revised condition.

(b) Determine the adequacy of the existing glulam girder for the final revised condition.

(c) Determine the adequacy of the new bolts in the new tension rod connection shown in **Figure 604E** for a 35-kip tension force.

604. **(Continued)**

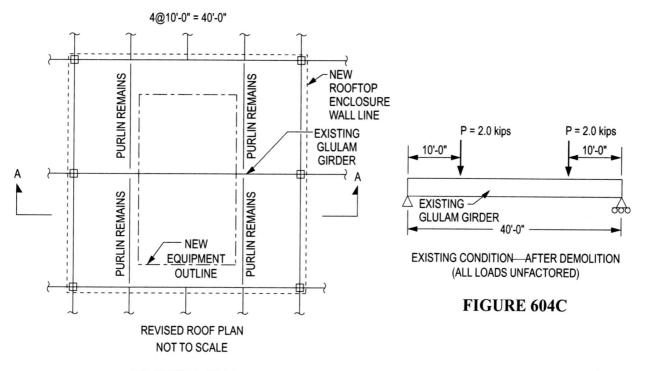

4@10'-0" = 40'-0"

PURLIN REMAINS

NEW ROOFTOP ENCLOSURE WALL LINE

EXISTING GLULAM GIRDER

NEW EQUIPMENT OUTLINE

A

REVISED ROOF PLAN
NOT TO SCALE

FIGURE 604A

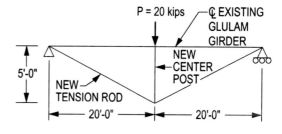

P = 2.0 kips   P = 2.0 kips

10'-0"   10'-0"

EXISTING GLULAM GIRDER

40'-0"

EXISTING CONDITION—AFTER DEMOLITION
(ALL LOADS UNFACTORED)

FIGURE 604C

P = 20 kips   ₵ EXISTING GLULAM GIRDER

NEW CENTER POST

5'-0"

NEW TENSION ROD

20'-0"   20'-0"

NEW EQUIPMENT LOAD
(ALL LOADS UNFACTORED)

FIGURE 604D

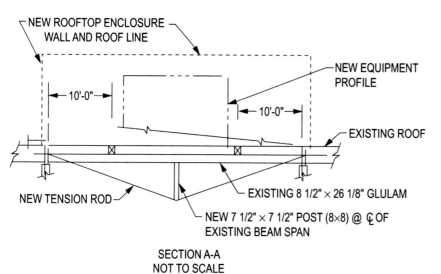

NEW ROOFTOP ENCLOSURE WALL AND ROOF LINE

NEW EQUIPMENT PROFILE

10'-0"

10'-0"

EXISTING ROOF

NEW TENSION ROD

EXISTING 8 1/2" × 26 1/8" GLULAM

NEW 7 1/2" × 7 1/2" POST (8×8) @ ₵ OF EXISTING BEAM SPAN

SECTION A-A
NOT TO SCALE

FIGURE 604B

604. **(Continued)**

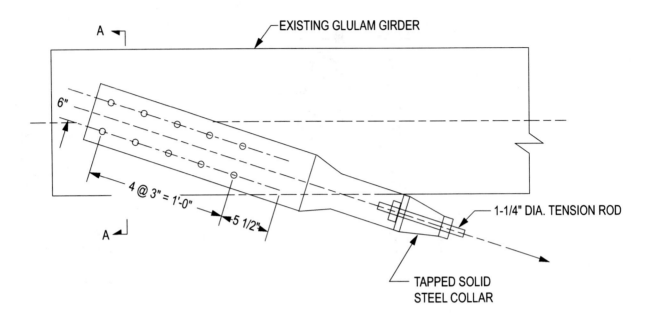

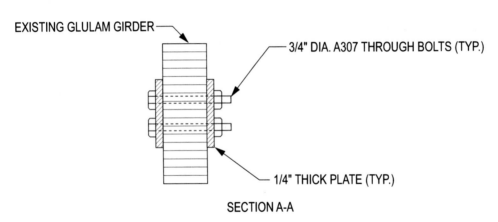

SECTION A-A

FIGURE 604E

604. (Continued)

TABLE 604A

Glulam 8 1/2 × 26 1/8 24F-1.7E	
$F_{b^+_{x\,(\text{tension zone in tension})}}$	2,400 psi
$F_{b^-_{x\,(\text{compression zone in tension})}}$	1,450 psi
$F_{c_{\perp x}}$	500 psi
F_{v_x}	210 psi
F_t	775 psi
F_c	1,000 psi
E_x	1.7×10^6 psi
E_{axial}	1.37×10^6 psi
$E_{x_{min}}$	0.9×10^6 psi
E_y	1.3×10^6 psi
$E_{y_{min}}$	0.69×10^6 psi
G	0.55
Adjustment Factors $C_D = 0.90$ $C_M = 1.0$ $C_t = 1.0$ $C_g = 0.95$ $C_L = 0.98$ $C_\Delta = 1.0$	

This completes the afternoon session. Solutions begin on page 91.

VERTICAL FORCES PM BRIDGES PRACTICE EXAM

701. **Figure 701** shows the elevation and cross sections of an interior prestressed concrete girder for a 120-ft-long, simple single-span highway bridge. The girders spaced on 5'-6" centers are composite with a 7 1/2-in. concrete slab. Each girder is prestressed with 34 strands, 8 of which are draped as shown. All strands are 1/2-in. nominal-diameter low-relaxation strands and prestressed to their allowable limits. Live load moments and shears are shown in **Table 701**.

Design Specification:
   AASHTO LRFD Bridge Design Specifications, 6th edition, 2012.

Design Data:
Concrete slab, f'_c	4 ksi
Concrete prestressed girders, f'_c	6 ksi
Density of concrete	0.150 kcf
Ductility factor	1.0
Redundancy factor	1.0
Importance factor	1.0
Low-relaxation 1/2-in.-diameter strands, f_{pu}	270 ksi
Area of 1/2-in.-diameter strands, A_s	0.153 in^2 per strand
Reinforcing bars, f_y	60 ksi
Dead load of the girder and slab, DC	1.30 kips/ft per girder
Superimposed dead load, DW	0.26 kips/ft per girder

Prestressed Girder Properties:
Cross-sectional area, A_g	713 in^2
Moment of inertia, I_g	392,638 in^4
Neutral axis to bottom fiber	32.12 in.
Neutral axis to top fiber	30.88 in.
Section modulus (bottom), S_{ncb}	12,224 in^3
Section modulus (top) S_{nct}	12,715 in^3

Composite Section Properties:
Cross-sectional area, A_g	1,117 in^2
Moment of inertia, I_c	704,000 in^4
Neutral axis to bottom fiber	44.64 in.
Section modulus (bottom), S_{cb}	15,767 in^3
Section modulus (top) S_{ct}	38,365 in^3
Effective slab width	66 in.

Assumptions:
   Total strand prestress loss is 40.5 ksi.
   For simplicity, the support centerlines are to be considered at the end faces of the girder.
   All strands are fully bonded.
   There is no nonprestressed tension or compression reinforcement.
   Section is in tension-controlled region.

701. **(Continued)**

TABLE 701

Maximum Live Load Moment per Girder (Dynamic Allowance Included) at 10th Points from a Support						
Location from support (ft)	0.0	0.1L	0.2L	0.3L	0.4L	0.5L
Maximum live load moment (ft-kips)	0	681	1,201	1,560	1,772	1,830

REQUIREMENTS:

On the actual exam, any sketches necessary for these requirements must be neatly drawn in your solution pamphlet.

(a) Verify the flexural adequacy for Strength I Limit State of the composite girder at midspan, including checking for minimum reinforcement. Assume rectangular section behavior.

(b) Determine anchorage zone vertical web reinforcement for the girder, using #5 bars, and show them on a sketch.

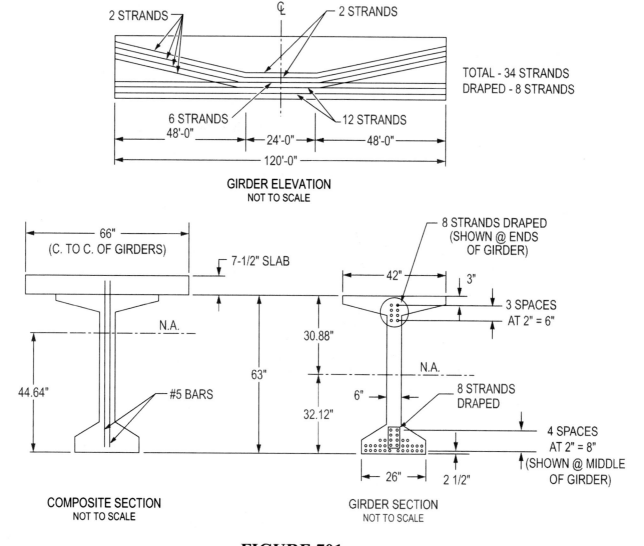

GIRDER ELEVATION
NOT TO SCALE

COMPOSITE SECTION
NOT TO SCALE

GIRDER SECTION
NOT TO SCALE

FIGURE 701

63   GO ON TO THE NEXT PAGE

702. **Figure 702** shows a bridge superstructure cross section. The bridge is a single-span structure with precast, prestressed concrete girders, a cast-in-place concrete deck, and a bituminous wearing surface. Barriers are cast-in-place.

Design Specification:
AASHTO LRFD Bridge Design Specifications, 6th edition, 2012.

Design Data:

Concrete unit weight, γ_c	0.150 kcf (precast and cast-in-place concrete)
Wearing surface unit weight	0.140 kcf
Bridge skew	0°
Bridge length	120'-0" (centerline of bearing to centerline of bearing)

Girder Properties:

f'_c	7 ksi
Weight	0.50 klf
I	265,320 in^4
A	570 in^2
e_g	28 in.

Cast-In-Place Properties:

f'_c	4 ksi

Assumptions:
Bridge barrier and wearing surface are applied evenly to all girders.
Ignore design tandem loading.
Superstructure is a conventionally redundant system.
Bridge is considered operationally important.

REQUIREMENTS:

(a) Determine permanent load moments M_{DC} and M_{DW} at midspan of Girder A.

(b) Determine maximum live load plus dynamic load allowance moment per lane at midspan of Girder A.

(c) Determine appropriate live load moment distribution factors for the applicable number of loaded lanes (include checks of applicability) for Girder A.

(d) Determine maximum moment, at midspan of Girder A, for the Strength I limit state.

702. **(Continued)**

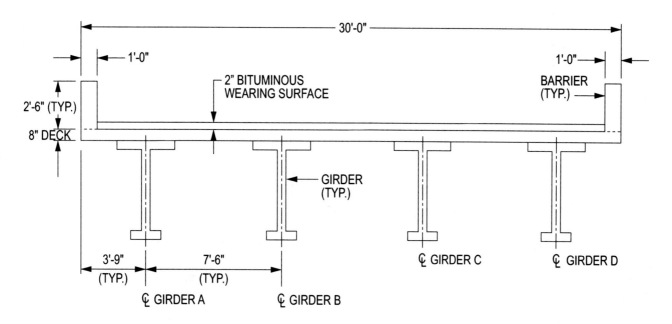

FIGURE 702

703. **Figure 703A** shows the elevation of a typical interior girder from a three-span continuous bridge on a major highway. The girders are all W36 × 231 standard sections. To facilitate the fabrication and erection of the girders, two field splices must be used. A preliminary design of the two symmetric splices at Points C results in 5/8-in. flange plates with 16 bolts on each side of the splice and 1/2-in. web plates with 30 bolts on each side of the splice. **Figure 703B** shows a plan and elevation of the preliminary splice design.

Design Specification:
   AASHTO LRFD Bridge Design Specifications, 6th edition, 2012.

Design Data:
   Load Resistance Factor Design (LRFD) is to be used.
   All steel is specified as AASHTO M-270, Grade 36.
   Bolts are specified as 7/8-in. diameter, AASHTO M-164 (ASTM A-325).
   Unfactored HL-93 design loading results in the following forces at the splices:

Force	DC	DW	Min LL+I *	Max LL+I *
Moment (ft-kips)	−69	26	−374	730
Shear (kips)	41	11	6	61

   *Minimum moments cause tension in the top flange of the girder and maximum moments cause tension in the bottom of the girder. Includes Multiple Presence Factor 3.6.1.1.2-1.

The AISC *Steel Construction Manual,* 13th edition, gives the following properties for a W36 × 231 section:

Area of section, A	68.1 in^2
Moment of inertia about x axis, I_x	15,600 in^4
Width of flange, b_f	16.5 in.
Thickness of flange, t_f	1.26 in.
Depth of section, d	36.5 in.
Thickness of web, t_w	0.76 in.

Assumptions:
   Ignore fatigue.
   In the region of the splice, the steel girder is not composite with the concrete deck.
   Web and flange bolt threads are not excluded from the shear planes.
   Assume Class A surface condition for splice design.
   Girder clear gap at splice is 1/4 in. maximum.

REQUIREMENTS:

Prepare the final design of the splice at Points C as follows:

(a) Verify the plate size for the flange splice (neglect the block shear).

(b) Verify the number of bolts in the flange splice.

Note: These verifications must address all significant design factors.

703. **(Continued)**

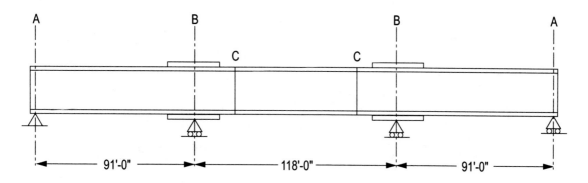

GIRDER ELEVATION

FIGURE 703A

703. **(Continued)**

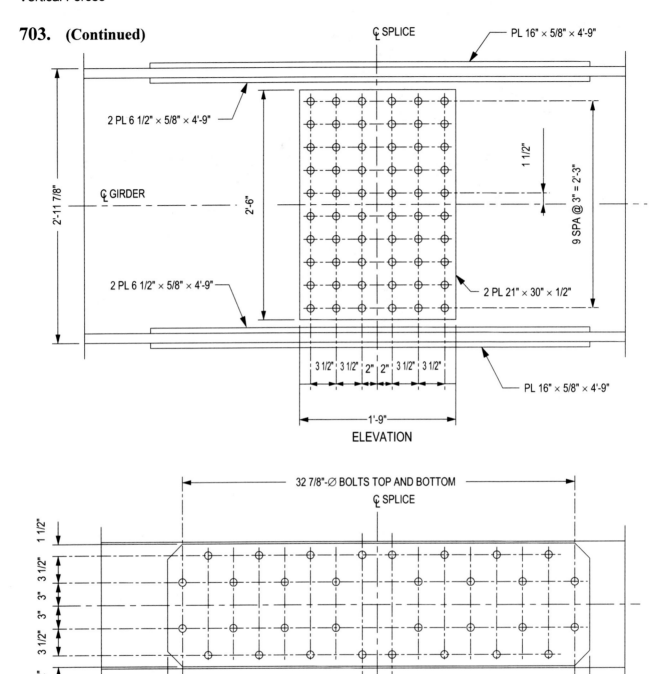

ELEVATION

PLAN

FIGURE 703B

This completes the afternoon session. Solutions begin on page 111.

Correct Answers to the AM Vertical Forces Practice Exam

Detailed solutions for each question begin on the next page.

101	C	121	C
102	C	122	B
103	C	123	C
104	D	124	A
105	C	125	C
106	B	126	B
107	A	127	D
108	D	128	C
109	D	129	C
110	A	130	C
111	D	131	B
112	A	132	A
113	C	133	A
114	B	134	B
115	B	135	D
116	B	136	C
117	A	137	D
118	B	138	D
119	B	139	B
120	C	140	D

101. Due to symmetry, the loads at each pier will be equal.

$$\Delta pier = \varepsilon_{sh}\frac{L}{2} + \alpha T \frac{L}{2}$$

$$\Delta pier = 0.0002(\frac{120}{2} \times 12) + 0.000006(40)(\frac{120}{2} \times 12)$$

$$= 0.32 \text{ in.}$$

For fixed-pin condition, $\Delta = \frac{Ph^3}{3EI}$; Solve for $P = \frac{3EI\Delta}{h^3}$

$$\therefore P = \frac{3(3,605 \text{ kips/in}^2)(636,000 \text{ in}^4)(0.32 \text{ in.})}{(20 \times 12 \text{ in.})^3} = 159 \text{ kips}$$

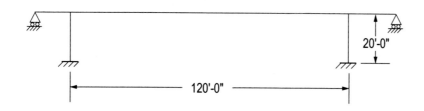

THE CORRECT ANSWER IS: (C)

102. w = (0.64 kips/ft)/lane   AASHTO Art. 3.6.1.2

$$M_{LL} = 0.64 \times \frac{35^2}{8} = 98 \text{ ft-kips/lane}$$

IM = 1.33   AASHTO Table 3.6.2.1-1

$$M_{LL+I} = 1.75(1.33 \times 360 \text{ ft-kips} + 98 \text{ ft-kips}) = 1,010 \text{ ft-kips}$$

THE CORRECT ANSWER IS: (C)

103. ASCE 7-10, Figure 7-9 Formula.

$$h_d = 0.43 \sqrt[3]{l_u} \sqrt[4]{p_g + 10} - 1.5$$

$$p_g = 30, \qquad l_u = 100 \text{ ft} \qquad \text{(given)}$$

$$h_d = 0.43 \sqrt[3]{100} \sqrt[4]{30 + 10} - 1.5 = 3.52 \text{ ft}$$

THE CORRECT ANSWER IS: (C)

104. ASCE 7-10, 4.9 Crane loads.

Wheel load	= 5 kips, cab operated.
Vertical force	= 1.0 P
Vertical impact force	= 0.25 P
Longitudinal force	= 0.1 P

Sec. 4.9.3

Sec. 4.9.5

$P_V = (1.0 + 0.25) \times 5 \text{ kips} = 6.25 \text{ kips}$

$P_H = 0.10 \times 5 \text{ kips} \quad = 0.5 \text{ kips}$

THE CORRECT ANSWER IS: (D)

105. By symmetry, $Y_A = Y_C = 10 \, W = 700 \text{ lb}$

$\sum M \text{ at } B = 0 \qquad Y_C \times 10 - W \times 10 \times \dfrac{10}{2} - T \times 5 = 0$

$\qquad\qquad\qquad T = 700 \text{ lb}$

Moment at Point D

$Y_C \times 5 - W \times 5 \times \dfrac{5}{2} - M = 0$

$700 \times 5 - 70 \times 5 \times \dfrac{5}{2} \quad = M$

$\therefore M = 2{,}625 \text{ ft-lb}$

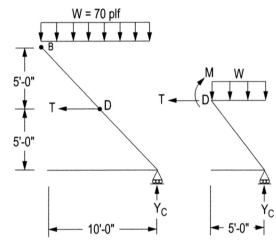

THE CORRECT ANSWER IS: (C)

106. AASHTO Table A4-1.

With span of 9'-6", $M_{L-L} = 7.15$ ft-kips

THE CORRECT ANSWER IS: (B)

107. Options B, C, and D show plates that connect at the midside nodes. Option A has a denser grid at the point load and all elements are connected at corner nodes.

THE CORRECT ANSWER IS: (A)

108. Because required shear/moments are at face of elements, simplified shear-moment diagrams can be used.

$V_1 = 0 - 10 = -10$ kips

$V_2 = -10 + 12.8 - 1.5 = 1.3$ kips

$V_{ab} = 1.3$ kips

$V_3 = 1.3 - 1.0 = 0.3$ kip

$V_{ba} = 0.3$ kip

$V_4 = 0.3 - 17 - 2 + 18.7 = 0.0$ kip

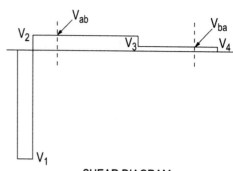

SHEAR DIAGRAM

Calculate moments from shear diagram:

$M_{ab} = (1.3 \text{ kips})(2 \text{ ft})(-10 \text{ kips})(1.5 \text{ ft}) = -12.4$ ft-kips

$M_{ba} = 0 - (0.3 \text{ kip})(2 \text{ ft}) = -0.6$ ft-kip

THE CORRECT ANSWER IS: (D)

109. Influence line for shear at right side of B:

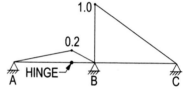

V_{B_R} from uniform load = area under influence line $\times$ w

V_{B_R} from point load = maximum value of influence line $\times$ P

$V_{B_R} = (1/2)(0.2)(60 \text{ ft})(1.0 \text{ klf}) + (1/2)(1.0)(60 \text{ ft})(1.0 \text{ klf}) + (1.0)(10 \text{ kips})$

$= 46.0$ kips

THE CORRECT ANSWER IS: (D)

110. Distribution factor $= \dfrac{K}{\sum K \text{ of joint}}$

$K = \dfrac{EI}{L}$ where E is constant

$K_{AB} = \dfrac{200}{20} = 10$

$K_{BC} = \dfrac{300}{15} = 20$

$DF_{B-A} = \dfrac{10}{10 + 20} = 0.33$

$DF_{B-C} = \dfrac{20}{10 + 20} = 0.67$

THE CORRECT ANSWER IS: (A)

111. Option A incorrectly uses constant shear in Span 1. Option B is incorrect because it uses the moment diagram for overhang. Option C is incorrect because it uses the inverted shear diagram for Span 1.

THE CORRECT ANSWER IS: (D)

112. The maximum moment at A occurs when a unit load is applied at the hinge. The moment at A will be zero when the unit load is at A or C.

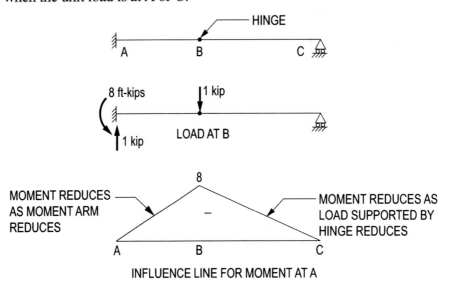

THE CORRECT ANSWER IS: (A)

113. $P_r = \phi P_n \geq P_u$ AASHTO 5.7.5 – 1

$P_n = 0.85\, f_c' A_1 m$ AASHTO 5.7.5 – 2

$m = \sqrt{\dfrac{A_2}{A_1}} \leq 2.0$ $A_2 = A_1$ due to lack of edge distance

$A = 11 \times W$

$\phi = 0.70$ bearing on concrete   AASHTO 5.5.4.2.1

$0.70\,[0.85\, f_c'\,(11)\,W \times m] \geq P_u$

$W \geq \dfrac{P_u}{0.7(0.85)f_c'(11)m}$

$m = 1.0$

$W = \dfrac{415}{0.7(0.85)(4.0)(11)(1.0)} = 15.9$ in.

THE CORRECT ANSWER IS: (C)

114. When concrete is placed on a hot, windy day, it is not permissible to add field water as needed to obtain the desired consistency and workability.

THE CORRECT ANSWER IS: (B)

115. $M_u = 1.25(1,200) + 1.5(100) + 1.75(850)$ AASHTO Table 3.4.1-1 and Table 3.4.1-2
$= 3,138$ ft-kips

THE CORRECT ANSWER IS: (B)

116. Report the condition to the contractor. Taking care of unsafe conditions is the contractor's responsibility.

THE CORRECT ANSWER IS: (B)

117. $I_y = 4[3.00 + 1.93(1.08 + 0.375)^2] + \dfrac{14(0.75)^3}{12} = 28.8 \text{ in}^4$

$A \quad = 4(1.93) + 14(0.75) = 18.2 \text{ in}^2$

$r_y \quad = \sqrt{28.8/18.2} = 1.26 \text{ in.}$

$\dfrac{Kl}{r_y} \quad = \dfrac{1.0(10)(12)}{1.26} = 95.2$

From Table 4-22 on page 4-324

$F_{cr}/\Omega_c = 13.4 \text{ ksi}$ $\phi_c F_{cr} = 20.1 \text{ ksi}$

$F_{cr} \quad = 13.4 \times 1.67 = 22.4 \text{ ksi}$ $F_{cr} \quad = 20.1/0.9 = 22.3 \text{ ksi}$

Alternate solution:

$F_{cr} \quad = [0.658^{F_y/F_e}]F_y$ because $\dfrac{Kl}{r} < 4.71\sqrt{\dfrac{E}{F_y}} = 133.7$

$F_e \quad = \dfrac{\pi^2 E}{\left(\dfrac{Kl}{r}\right)^2} = 31.6 \text{ ksi}$

$F_{cr} = 22.3 \text{ ksi}$

THE CORRECT ANSWER IS: (A)

118. Strength I, $M_u = 1.25(25.8 \text{ ft-kips}) + 1.75(492.7 \text{ ft-kips}) = 894.5 \text{ ft-kips}$ AASHTO 6.13

$F_{nc} = F_{nt} = R_h F_y$ of smaller of the two sections (W36 × 135, $S_x = 439 \text{ in}^3$)

$R_h = 1.0$ since all steel is 50 ksi; $F_n = 1.0(50 \text{ ksi}) = 50 \text{ ksi}$

$\phi f = 1.0$ AASHTO 6.5.4.2

$M_{rx} = \phi_f F_{nc} S_{xc} = 1.00(50 \text{ ksi})(439 \text{ in}^3)\dfrac{1}{12} = 1{,}829 \text{ ft-kips}$ (C.6.8.2.3.1)

Design connection for average $= \dfrac{894.5 \text{ ft-kips} + 1{,}829 \text{ ft-kips}}{2} = 1{,}362 \text{ ft-kips}$ AASHTO 6.13.1

or $= 0.75(1{,}829 \text{ ft-kips}) = 1{,}372 \text{ ft-kips}$ Controls

THE CORRECT ANSWER IS: (B)

119. The DL carried by the steel section for unshored construction is self-weight and wet weight of concrete. See AISC I3-1b.

$$M_{DL} = \frac{wL^2}{8}$$

$$= 0.676\left(\frac{60^2}{8}\right) = 304 \text{ ft-kips}$$

THE CORRECT ANSWER IS: (B)

120. **ASD option:**

Load combination: $D + 0.75L_r + 0.45W$

$P = 7.2 + 0.75(12.6) + 0.45(6.4) = 19.53 \text{ kips}$

W14 × 53 $A = 15.6 \text{ in}^2$

$r_x = 5.89 \text{ in.}$

$r_y = 1.92 \text{ in.}$

$$\frac{K_x L}{r_x} = \frac{2.0(15 \times 12)}{5.89} = 61.1$$

$$\frac{K_y L}{r_y} = \frac{1.0(15 \times 12)}{1.92} = 93.8 \quad \text{Controls}$$

120. **(Continued)**

$F_{cr} / \Omega = 15.7 \text{ ksi}$ AISC Table 4 - 22

$P_c = F_{cr}A_g = 15.7(15.6) = 245 \text{ kips}$

$\dfrac{P_r}{P_c} = \dfrac{19.53}{245} = 0.08 < 0.2 \rightarrow \text{Use AISC Eq. H1-1b}$

So AISC Eq. H1-1b,

$$\frac{P_r}{2\,P_c} + \left(\frac{M_{rx}}{M_{cx}} + \frac{M_{ry}}{M_{cy}}\right) = \frac{19.53}{2\,(245)} + \frac{113}{173} = 0.040 + 0.653 = 0.693$$

LRFD option:

Load combination: $1.2\,D + 1.6\,L_r + 0.5W$

$P_r = 1.2\,(7.2) + 1.6\,(12.6) + 0.5\,(6.4) = 32.0 \text{ kips}$

W14 × 53 $A = 15.6 \text{ in}^2$

$r_x = 5.89 \text{ in.}$

$r_x = 1.92 \text{ in.}$

$\dfrac{K_x L}{r_x} = \dfrac{2.0\,(15 \times 12)}{5.89} = 61.1$

$\dfrac{K_y L}{r_y} = \dfrac{1.0\,(15 \times 12)}{1.92} = 93.8$ Controls

$\varnothing\,F_{cr} = 23.6 \text{ ksi}$ AISC Table 4-22

$P_c = F_{cr}\,A_g = 23.6\,(15.6) = 368 \text{ kips}$

$\dfrac{P_r}{P_c} = \dfrac{32.0}{368} = 0.09 < 0.2 \quad \rightarrow \quad \text{Use AISC Eq. H1-1b}$

So AISC Eq. H1-1b,

$$\frac{P_r}{2P_c} + \left(\frac{M_{rx}}{M_{cx}} + \frac{M_{ry}}{M_{cy}}\right) = \frac{32.0}{2(368)} + \frac{180}{262}$$

$$= 0.043 + 0.687 = 0.730$$

THE CORRECT ANSWER IS: (C)

121. For a W14 × 53 column, $d = 13.9$ in. and $b_f = 8.06$ in.

p. 1-24

From p. 14–5:

$$m = \frac{16 - 0.95\,(13.9)}{2} = 1.40$$

Eq. 14-2

$$n = \frac{10 - 0.8\,(8.06)}{2} = 1.78$$

Eq. 14-3

$$n' = \frac{\sqrt{13.9 \times 8.06}}{4} = 2.65$$

Eq. 14-4

ASD option:

$$\frac{P_n}{\Omega_c} @ 12\ \text{ft} = 365\ \text{kips}$$

p. 4-20

$$\frac{4\,d b_f}{(d + b_f)^2} = 0.929$$

Eq. 14-6b

$$X = 0.929 \times \frac{150}{365} = 0.382$$

$$\lambda = \frac{2\sqrt{X}}{1 + \sqrt{1 - X}} = 0.692$$

Eq. 14-5

$$\lambda n' = 0.692 \times 2.65 = 1.83\ \text{in.}$$

$$\ell = \text{larger}\ (1.40,\ 1.78,\ 1.83) = 1.83\ \text{in.}$$

$$t_{min} = \ell \sqrt{\frac{3.33 P_a}{F_y BN}} = 1.83 \sqrt{\frac{3.33(150)}{36(10)(16)}}$$

Eq. 14-7b

$$= 0.54\ \text{in.} \rightarrow \text{use}\ 5/8\ \text{in.}$$

121. (Continued)

LRFD option:

$\phi_c P_n$ @ 12 ft = 549 kips   p. 4-20

$$\frac{4db_f}{(d+b_f)^2} = 0.929$$ Eq. 14-6a

$$X = 0.929 \times \frac{190 \text{ kips}}{549 \text{ kips}} = 0.322$$

$$\lambda = \frac{2\sqrt{X}}{1+\sqrt{1-X}} = 0.622$$

$\lambda n' = 0.622 \times 2.65 = 1.65$

ℓ = larger (1.40, 1.78, 1.65) = 1.78 in.

$$t_{min} = \ell\sqrt{\frac{2P_u}{0.9\,F_y BN}} = 1.78\sqrt{\frac{2(190 \text{ kips})}{(0.9)(36 \text{ ksi})(10)(16)}}$$ Eq. 14-7a

$= 0.482 \rightarrow$ Use 1/2 in.

THE CORRECT ANSWER IS: (C)

122. ASD option:

$M_n = S_e F_y$ Eq. C3.1.1-1

$$M_n = \frac{2(0.812)(33)(1,000)}{12} = 4,466 \text{ ft-lb}$$

$$\frac{M_n}{\Omega_b} = \frac{4,466 \text{ ft-lb}}{1.67} = 2,674 \text{ ft-lb}$$

LRFD option:

$M_n = S_e F_y$ Eq. C3.1.1-1

$$M_n = \frac{2(0.812)(33)(1,000)}{12} = 4,466 \text{ ft-lb}$$

$\phi_b M_n = 0.95(4,466) = 4,243 \text{ ft-lb}$

THE CORRECT ANSWER IS: (B)

123. M due to girder weight $= (0.822)\left(\dfrac{76^2}{8}\right) = 594\,\text{ft-kips}$

$f_t = \dfrac{P}{A} - \dfrac{P}{S_t}$ (distance from center of strands to the C.G. of girder) $+ \dfrac{M_{DL}}{S_t}$

$= \dfrac{650}{789} - \dfrac{650(24.73-4)}{8{,}089} + \dfrac{(594)(12)}{8{,}089} = 0.039\,\text{ksi, compression}$

$f_b = \dfrac{650}{789} + \dfrac{650(20.73)}{10{,}543} - \dfrac{(594)(12)}{10{,}543} = 1.426\,\text{ksi, compression}$

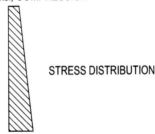

0.039 ksi, COMPRESSION

STRESS DISTRIBUTION

1.426 ksi, COMPRESSION

THE CORRECT ANSWER IS: (C)

124. Per ACI 318-11 3.3.2

Size of coarse aggregate shall be not larger than:

1. 1/5 member width $= \dfrac{1}{5} \times 10 = 2"$

2. 1/3 slab depth $= \dfrac{1}{3} \times 5 = 1.67"$

3. 3/4 minimum clear spacing between individual rebars
   Total space $= 10" - 2(0.75") - 2(0.5") - 4(0.75") = 4.5"$
   Clear spacing $= 4.5"/3 = 1.5"$
   $3/4 \times$ clear spacing $= 1.125"$ Controls

THE CORRECT ANSWER IS: (A)

125.
$$d_e = d_s = 60 - 1.5 - \frac{1.128}{2} - 0.625 = 57.31 \text{ in.}$$

$$a = \frac{A_s f_y}{0.85\, f_c'\, b} = \frac{10 \times 1.00 \times 60}{0.85 \times 4 \times 36} = 4.902 \text{ in.}$$

$$\therefore d_v = d_e - \frac{a}{2} = 57.31 - \frac{4.902}{2}$$

$$= 54.86 \text{ in.} \qquad \text{Controls}$$

$$0.9\, d_e = 51.58 \text{ in.} < 54.86 \text{ in.}$$

$$0.72\, h = 43.2 \text{ in.} < 54.86 \text{ in.}$$

AASHTO 5.8.2.9

THE CORRECT ANSWER IS: (C)

126.
$$I_{beam} = (0.35)(11,000) = 3,850 \text{ in}^4$$

$$I_{col} = (0.70)(5,460) = 3,822 \text{ in}^4$$

$$\sum \frac{EI_{col}}{L} = \frac{(2)(3,822)}{13.67} = 559 \quad \text{(Neglect E for } f_c'; \text{ same for beams and columns.)}$$

$$\sum \frac{EI_{beam}}{L_c} = \frac{(2)(3,850)}{20} = 385$$

$$\Psi_A = \Psi_B = \frac{559}{385} = 1.45$$

From ACI 318-11, Figure R10.10.1.1 (b), k = 1.45

THE CORRECT ANSWER IS: (B)

127. l_{dc} $= \left(\dfrac{0.02\, f_y}{\lambda \sqrt{f'_c}} \right) d_b$ ACI 12.3.2

$$= \dfrac{(0.02)(60,000)(1.41)}{(1.0)\sqrt{4,000}} = 26.8 \text{ in.}$$

Check l_{dc} $= (0.0003\, f_y)\, d_b$

$= 0.0003(60,000)(1.41)$

$= 25.4 \ < \ 26.8$

26.8 in. governs

THE CORRECT ANSWER IS: (D)

128. Reference bolt design value, $Z_\parallel = 1,870$ lb Table 11F

THE CORRECT ANSWER IS: (C)

129. **ASD option:**

$M'_r \ = F'_b \, S_{xx} = (1,219 \text{ psi})(21.39 \text{ in}^3) = 26,080 \text{ in-lb}$

where :

$F'_b \ = F_b C_D C_L C_F C_r [\underbrace{C_M C_t C_{fu} C_i}_{1.0}]$

$= (850 \text{ psi})(1.15)(0.986)(1.1)(1.15) = 1,219 \text{ psi}$

$F_b = 850$ psi Table 4A

$C_D = 1.15$ for snow Table 2.3.2

$C_L = 0.986$ Given

$C_F = 1.1$ Table 4A

$C_r = 1.15$ Table 4A

$S_{xx} = 1/6\, bh^2 = (1.5 \text{ in.})(9.25 \text{ in.})^2 / 6 = 21.39 \text{ in}^3$ Table 1B

129. **(Continued)**

LRFD option:

$M_r' = F_b' S_{xx} = (1,831 \text{ psi})(21.39 \text{ in}^3) = 39,170 \text{ in.-lb}$

where :

$$F_b' = F_b C_L C_F C_r K_F \phi_b \lambda \underbrace{[C_M C_t C_{fu} C_i]}_{1.0}$$

$= (850 \text{ psi})(0.986)(1.1)(1.15)(2.54)(0.85)(0.8) = 1,831 \text{ psi}$

$F_b = 850 \text{ psi}$	Table 4A
$C_L = 0.986$	Given
$C_F = 1.1$	Table 4A
$C_r = 1.15$	Table 4A
$K_F = 2.54$	Table 4.3.1
$\phi_b = 0.85$	Table 4.3.1
$\lambda = 0.8$	Given
$S_{xx} \, 1/6 \, bh^2 = (1.5 \text{ in.})(9.25 \text{ in.})^2/6 = 21.39 \text{ in}^3$	Table 1B

THE CORRECT ANSWER IS: (C)

130. $3 \, 1/8 \times 12 \, 3/8 \quad S_X = 79.76 \text{ in}^3$ Table 1D, p. 22

     $24F - E1 \qquad SP/SP \qquad F_{bx}^+ = 2,400 \text{ psi}$ Table 5A, p. 63

                         $F_{bx}^- = 1,450 \text{ psi}$ (Use for negative moment at post)

ASD option:

$$M_n' = \frac{79.76 \times 1,450}{1,000 \times 12} = 9.6 \text{ ft-kips}$$

LRFD option:

$$M_n' = \frac{79.76 \times 1,450 \times 2.54 \times 0.85 \times 0.8}{1,000 \times 12} = 16.7 \text{ ft-kips}$$

THE CORRECT ANSWER IS: (C)

131. **ASD option:**

$$F_c' = F_c C_p [\underbrace{C_D C_M C_t C_F C_i}_{1.0}] = (1,000 \text{ psi})(1.0)(0.67) = 670 \text{ psi}$$

$F_c = 1,000 \text{ psi}$ Table 4D

$$C_P = \frac{1 + (F_{cE}/F_c^*)}{2c} - \sqrt{\left[\frac{1 + (F_{cE}/F_c^*)}{2c}\right]^2 - \frac{(F_{cE}/F_c^*)}{c}} = 0.67 \qquad \text{Eq. 3.7-1}$$

$\dfrac{F_{cE}}{F_c^*} = 0.957$ Given

$c = 0.8$ Sawn lumber   Sec. 3.7.1

LRFD option:

$$F_c' = F_c C_p K_F \phi_c \lambda [\underbrace{C_M C_t C_F C_i}_{1.0}] = (1,000 \text{ psi})(0.67)(2.40)(0.90)(0.80) = 1,160 \text{ psi}$$

$F_c = 1,000 \text{ psi}$ Table 4D

$$C_P = \frac{1 + (F_{cE}/F_c^*)}{2c} - \sqrt{\left[\frac{1 + (F_{cE}/F_c^*)}{2c}\right]^2 - \frac{(F_{cE}/F_c^*)}{c}} = 0.67 \qquad \text{Eq. 3.7-1}$$

$\dfrac{F_{cE}}{F_c^*} = 0.957$ Given

$c = 0.8$ Sawn lumber   Sec. 3.7.1

THE CORRECT ANSWER IS: (B)

132. **ASD option:**

$B_{ab} = 1.25 \, A_{pt} \sqrt{f_m'}$ Eq. 2-3

$A_{pt} = \pi \ell_b^2$ Eq. 1-4

$\ell_b = 6 \, 1/4" - 2(5/8") = 5"$ Sec. 1.17.5

$B_{ab} = 1.25(\pi)(5)^2 \sqrt{1,500} = 3,800 \text{ lb}$

$B_{ab} = 0.6 \, f_m' e_b d_b + 120 \, \pi(\ell_b + e_b + d_b) d_b$ Eq. 2-4

$e_b = 1 \, 7/8" - 5/8" = 1 \, 1/4"$ Sec. 1.4, p. C-8

$B_{ab} = 0.6(1,500)(1 \, 1/4")(5/8") + 120 \, (\pi)(5" + 1 \, 1/4" + 5/8")(5/8")$

$B_{ab} = 2,300 \text{ lb}$ Controls

$B_{as} = 0.6 \, A_b f_y$ Eq. 2-5

$B_{as} = 0.6(0.31)(36,000) = 6,700 \text{ lb}$

132. (Continued)

LRFD option:

$$\phi B_{anb} = \phi\, 4\, A_{pt} \sqrt{f'_m} \qquad\qquad \text{Eq. 3-3}$$

$$A_{pt} = \pi \ell_b^2 \qquad\qquad \text{Eq. 1-4}$$

$$\ell_b = 6\,1/4" - 2(5/8") = 5" \qquad\qquad \text{Sec. 1.17.5}$$

$$\phi = 0.50 \qquad\qquad \text{Sec. 3.1.4.1}$$

$$\phi B_{anb} = (0.50)(4)(\pi)(5)^2 \sqrt{1,500} = 6,100 \text{ lb}$$

$$\phi B_{anp} = \phi\left[1.5\, f'_m e_b d_b + 300\pi(\ell_b + e_b + d_b)d_b\right] \qquad\qquad \text{Eq. 3-4}$$

$$e_b = 1\,7/8" - 5/8" = 1\,1/4" \qquad\qquad \text{Sec. 1.4, p. c-8}$$

$$\phi = 0.65 \qquad\qquad \text{Sec. 3.1.4.1}$$

$$\phi B_{anp} = (0.65)\left[15(1,500)(1\,1/4")(5/8") + 300(\pi)(5" + 1\,1/4" + 5/8")(5/8")\right]$$

$$\phi B_{anp} = 3,800 \text{ lb} \qquad \text{Controls}$$

$$\phi B_{ans} = \phi A_b f_y \qquad\qquad \text{Eq. 3-5}$$

$$\phi = 0.90 \qquad\qquad \text{Sec. 3.1.4.1}$$

$$\phi B_{ans} = (0.9)(0.31)(36,000)$$

$$\phi B_{ans} = 1,000 \text{ lb}$$

THE CORRECT ANSWER IS: (A)

133. ASD option:

$$h = 144 \text{ in.} \qquad r = 2.66 \text{ in.} \qquad h/r = 54.1 < 99$$

$$P_a = (0.25\, f'_m A_n + 0.65\, A_{st}F_s)\left[1 - \left(\frac{h}{140\,r}\right)^2\right] \qquad\qquad \text{Eq. 2-21}$$

$$P_a = \left[0.25(1,500)(161) + 0.65\,(0.31)(32,000)\right]\left[1 - \left(\frac{54.1}{140}\right)^2\right]$$

$$P_a = 56,845 \text{ lb/4-ft length}$$

$$= 14,211 \text{ plf}$$

133. **(Continued)**

LRFD option:

$\qquad$ h = 144 in. $\qquad$ r = 2.66 in. $\qquad$ h/r = 54.1 < 99

$$\phi P_n = 0.80\left[0.80\, f'_m (A_n - A_{st}) + f_y A_{st}\right]\left[1 - \left(\frac{h}{140r}\right)^2\right] \qquad \text{Eq. 3-18}$$

$$\phi = 0.9 \qquad\qquad \text{Sec. 3.1.4.4}$$

$$\phi P_n = 0.9\left[0.8\left[0.80(1,500)(161 - 0.31) + (60,000)(0.31)\right]\left[1 - \left(\frac{54.1}{140}\right)^2\right]\right]$$

$\phi P_n = 129,546$ lb/4-ft length

$\qquad = 32,387$ plf

Note: equivalent masonry wall thickness is

$A_n = 48 \times 1.25 \times 2 + 5.125 \times 8 = 161$ in^2/4-ft length.

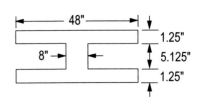

THE CORRECT ANSWER IS: (A)

134. Working Stress Design

$\qquad f'_m = 1,500$ psi

$$E_s = 29 \times 10^6 \qquad\qquad \text{Sec. 1.8.2.1}$$

$$E_m = 900\, f'_m \qquad\qquad \text{Sec. 1.8.2.2.1}$$

$$E_m = 900(1,500) = 1.35 \times 10^6 \text{ psi}$$

$$n = E_s/E_m = 29/1.35 = 21.5$$

$$\rho = A_s/bd = 0.31 / 48\left(\frac{7.625}{2}\right) = 0.0017$$

$$n\rho = 0.0366$$

$$k = \sqrt{n\rho^2 + 2n\rho} - n\rho = 0.236$$

$$j = 1 - k/3 = 0.921$$

$$F_b = 0.45\, f'_m = 675 \text{ psi} \qquad\qquad \text{Sec. 2.3.4.2.2}$$

$$M_{max} = F_b bkjd^2/[2(12)] = 675(12)(0.236)(0.921)(7.625/2)^2/[2(12)]$$

$\qquad = 1,070$ ft-lb/ft

THE CORRECT ANSWER IS: (B)

135.

I_{xx} pile group $= 4(4.5)^2 = 81$ pile-ft^2

I_{yy} pile group $= 6(2.25)^2 = 30.375$ pile-ft^2

Pile cap weight $= (7.5\text{ ft})(12.0\text{ ft})(3.0\text{ ft})(150\text{ pcf}) = 40.5$ kips

Maximum pile reaction $= \dfrac{250\text{ kips} + 40.5\text{ kips}}{6\text{ piles}} + \dfrac{(320\text{ ft-kips})(4.5\text{ ft})}{81\text{ pile-ft}^2} + \dfrac{(225\text{ ft-kips})(2.25\text{ ft})}{30.375\text{ pile-ft}^2}$

$\qquad = \quad 48.42 \quad + \quad 17.78 \quad + \quad 16.67$

$\qquad = 82.87$ kips

THE CORRECT ANSWER IS: (D)

136.

$g_c = \dfrac{P}{A} + \dfrac{M}{S}$

$g_t = \dfrac{P}{A} - \dfrac{M}{S}$

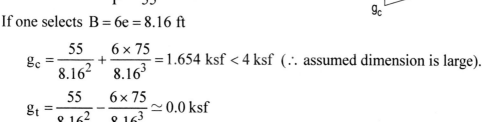

For a square footing with dimensions B × B

$A = B \times B$

$I = \dfrac{B^4}{12}, \ y = B/2, \ S = I/y = \dfrac{B^3}{6}$

Eccentricity, $e = \dfrac{M}{P} = \dfrac{75}{55} = 1.36$ ft

If one selects $B = 6e = 8.16$ ft

$g_c = \dfrac{55}{8.16^2} + \dfrac{6 \times 75}{8.16^3} = 1.654$ ksf $(\therefore$ assumed dimension is large).

$g_t = \dfrac{55}{8.16^2} - \dfrac{6 \times 75}{8.16^3} \simeq 0.0$ ksf

$\therefore$ One can select dimensions less than those above. In this case, g_t will be greater than zero. The stress distribution will look like the following. In this case the eccentric applied load must line up with the resultant of the compression stress beneath the footing, i.e.,

$B/2 = \dfrac{x}{3} + e$

$x = 3\left(\dfrac{B}{2} - e\right)$

and $P = \dfrac{1}{2}(g_b)(x)(B)$

$P = \dfrac{1}{2}g\left[3\left(\dfrac{B}{2} - \dfrac{M}{P}\right)\right] \times B$

$55 = \dfrac{1}{2} \times 4\left[3\left(\dfrac{B}{2} - 1.36\right)\right] \times B$

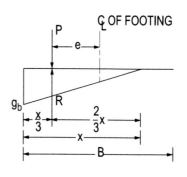

136. **(Continued)**

or

$$3B^2 - 8.16B - 55 = 0$$

$$B^2 - 2.72B - 18.333 = 0$$

$$B = 2.72 \pm \sqrt{\frac{2.72^2 - 4 \times 1 \times (-18.33)}{2}}$$

B = 5.853 ft   say 5.9 ft × 5.9 ft

THE CORRECT ANSWER IS: (C)

137. The most efficient footing and steel reinforcement will have the following:
- A larger heel than toe
- Heel reinforcement near the top face
- Toe reinforcement near the bottom face
- Wall reinforcing placed at face of high soil side

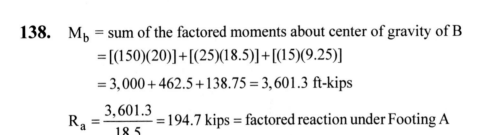

THE CORRECT ANSWER IS: (D)

138. M_b = sum of the factored moments about center of gravity of B

$$= [(150)(20)] + [(25)(18.5)] + [(15)(9.25)]$$

$$= 3,000 + 462.5 + 138.75 = 3,601.3 \text{ ft-kips}$$

$$R_a = \frac{3,601.3}{18.5} = 194.7 \text{ kips} = \text{factored reaction under Footing A}$$

M_a = factored moment sum about center of gravity of A

$$= [(-150)(1.5)] + [(200)(18.5)] + [(35)(18.5)] + [(15)(9.25)]$$

$$= -225 + 3,700 + 647.5 + 138.8 = 4,261.3 \text{ ft-kips}$$

$$R_b = \frac{4,261.3}{18.5} = 230.3 \text{ kips}$$

THE CORRECT ANSWER IS: (D)

139. W18 × 50 $I_x = 800\,\text{in}^4$

$A = 14.7\,\text{in}^2$

$d = 18\,\text{in.}$

1/2" plate $I_D = \dfrac{(6)(0.5)^3}{12} = 0.0625\,\text{in}^4$

$A = 6 \times 0.5 = 3\,\text{in}^2$

$\bar{y} = \dfrac{(14.7)(0.5 + \frac{18}{2}) + (3)(\frac{0.5}{2})}{14.7 + 3} = 7.93\,\text{in.}$

$I = [800 + (14.7)(0.5 + \frac{18}{2} - 7.93)^2] + [0.0625 + 3(7.93 - \frac{0.5}{2})^2] = 836 + 177 = 1{,}013\,\text{in}^4$

$Q = (3)(7.93 - \dfrac{0.5}{2}) = 23.04\,\text{in}^3$

$\dfrac{VQ}{I} = \dfrac{(40\,\text{kips})(23.04\,\text{in}^3)}{1{,}013\,\text{in}^4} = 0.91\,\text{kip/in.} = 10.92\,\text{kips/ft}$

$\dfrac{10.92\,\text{kips/ft}}{2.78\,\text{kips/in.}} = 3.93\,\text{in./ft}$ Use 2" at 12" each side of plate

THE CORRECT ANSWER IS: (B)

140. Options A, B, C are required per IBC Sec. 1704.3.1

THE CORRECT ANSWER IS: (D)

VERTICAL FORCES PM BUILDINGS SOLUTIONS

601. (a) CMU wall design

ASD solution:

$D + H + F + 0.75\,L + 0.75(L_r \text{ or } S \text{ or } R)$ IBC Eq. 16-11

Vertical Loads: Given $P_D = 980$ plf

$P_{LR} = 160 \times 0.75 = 120$ plf

$P_{LF} = 640 \times 0.75 = 480$ plf

Maximum stress in wall occurs at bottom of wall:

Wall weight $= 84$ psf (given) $\times 4.67$ ft $= 392$ plf

$P_{total} = 980 + 392 + 120 + 480 = 1{,}972$ lb/ft

Lateral loads: Surcharge:

(surcharge load live $= 100$ psf) $\times$

(active soil pressure coefficient $= 0.35$) $= 35$ psf

Active soil pressure:

(active pressure $= 0.35 \times 110$ pcf $= 38.5$ psf/ft) $\times$

(soil ht $= 4$ ft) $= 154$ psf

$\therefore$ moment at base $= (35 \text{ psf} \times 4 \text{ ft}) \times 2 \text{ ft} \left(\text{surcharge}\right) + \left(\dfrac{1}{2}\right)(154)(4 \text{ ft})\left(\dfrac{4 \text{ ft}}{3}\right)$ (active)

$= 280 + 411$

$= 691$ ft-lb/ft

Check compression:

$k = 2.1$ (fixed base and free top)

$r = t/\sqrt{12} = 7.625/\sqrt{12}$

$= 2.20$

$k\,h/r = \dfrac{2.1(4.67 \text{ ft})(12 \text{ in/ft})}{2.20} = 54 < 99$

Use Eq. 2-21(neglecting compressive stress in steel per Sec. 2.3.3.3): TMS 402, Sec. 2.3.4

$$P_a = (0.25 \times f'_m \times A_n)\left[1 - \left(\frac{h}{140\,r}\right)^2\right]$$

$f'_m = 2{,}000$ psi (given)

$A_n = 7.675 \text{ in.} \times 12 \text{ in/ft} = 91.5 \text{ in}^2/\text{ft}$

601. **(Continued)**

$$\therefore P_a = (0.25)(2,000)(91.5\,\text{in}^2/\text{ft})\left[1-\left(\frac{54}{140}\right)^2\right] = 38,944\,\text{lb/ft} > P_{\text{total}}$$

Check flexure:

$$A_{st} = 0.31\,\text{in}^2 \times \left(\frac{12\,\text{in.}}{32\,\text{in.}}\right) = 0.116\,\text{in}^2$$

$$E_m = 900\,f'_m = 1,800,000 \qquad\qquad \text{TMS 402-11, Sec. 1.8.2.2.1}$$

$$E_s = 29,000,000 \qquad\qquad\qquad\qquad \text{TMS 402-11, Sec. 1.8.2.1}$$

$$F_b = 0.45\,f'_m = 900\,\text{psi} \qquad\qquad\quad \text{TMS 402-11, Sec. 2.3.3.2.2}$$

$$n = \frac{E_s}{E_m} = \frac{29}{1.8} = 16.11 \qquad n\rho = \frac{A_{st} \times n}{b \times d} = \frac{(0.116\,\text{in}^2)(16.11)}{(12\,\text{in.})(5.25\,\text{in.})}$$

$$= 0.0297$$

$$k = \sqrt{2\rho n + (\rho n)^2} - \rho n$$

$$= 0.216$$

$$j = 1 - \frac{k}{3} = 0.928$$

$$M_{\text{allow}}\,(\text{steel}) = A_{st}F_s\,jd$$

$$= (0.116\,\text{in}^2/\text{ft})(32\,\text{ksi})(0.928)(5.25\,\text{in.}) = 18,085\,\frac{\text{in.-lb}}{\text{ft}} = 1,507\,\frac{\text{ft-lb}}{\text{ft}}$$

$$M_{\text{allow}}\,(\text{CMU}) = \frac{F_b\,jkbd^2}{2} = \frac{(900)(0.928)(0.216)(12)(5.25)^2}{2}$$

$$= 29,834\,\text{in.-lb/ft}$$

$$= 2,486\,\text{ft-lb/ft}$$

Steel stress controls   1,507 ft-lb > 691 ft-lb OK

Check combined stresses:

$$f_b = \frac{2M}{jkbd^2} = \frac{(2)(691\,\text{ft-lb} \times 12\,\text{in.}/\text{ft})}{(0.928)(0.216)(12\,\text{in.})(5.25)^2} = 250\,\text{psi}$$

$$f_a = \frac{1,972\,\text{lb/ft}}{(12\,\text{in.}/\text{ft})(7.625\,\text{in.})} = 22\,\text{psi}$$

per 2.3.4.2.2 $f_a + f_b < 0.45\,f'_m$

22 + 250 = 272 < 900

#5 @ 32 in., 8 in. CMU wall OK for loads

601. **(Continued)**

Strength Design Solution:

$$1.2(D + F) + 1.6(L + H) + 0.5(L_r \text{ or } S \text{ or } R)$$ IBC Eq. 16-2

Compression:
$$\begin{aligned} D &= 1.2 \times (980 + 392) &= 1{,}646 \text{ plf} \\ L &= 1.6 \times 640 &= 1{,}024 \text{ plf} \\ L_r &= 0.5 \times 160 &= 80 \text{ plf} \\ \text{Total} & &= 2{,}750 \text{ plf} \end{aligned}$$

Flexure: $$M_{L+H} = 1.6(280 + 411) = 1{,}106 \text{ ft-lb/ft}$$

Check compression: $$\frac{kh}{r} = \frac{(2.1)(4.67 \text{ ft})(12 \text{ in./ft})}{\left(7.625 / \sqrt{12}\right)} = 54 < 99$$

$\therefore$ Use TMS 402 Eq. 3-18 (Neglecting compressive stress in steel per Sec. 3.3.2(e))

$$P_n = 0.80\left[0.80 \, f'_m A_n\right]\left[1 - \left(\frac{h}{140\,r}\right)^2\right]$$

$$= 0.8\left[0.80(2{,}000)(7.625 \text{ in.} \times 12 \text{in./ft}\right]\left[1 - \left(\frac{54}{140}\right)^2\right]$$

$$= 99{,}695 \text{ lb}$$

$$\phi = 0.9$$ TMS 402, Sec. 3.1.4.4

$$\therefore \phi P_n = 89{,}726 \text{ plf} > 2{,}750 \text{ plf} \qquad \text{OK}$$

Check flexure:

$$d = 5.25 \text{ in.} \qquad \rho = \frac{A_{st}}{bd} = \frac{0.31(12/32)}{12(5.25 \text{ in.})} = 0.00185$$

$$\omega' = \rho \, f_y / f'_m = 0.00185\left(\frac{60}{2}\right) = 0.0555$$

$$\begin{aligned} M_n &= \omega' bd^2 f'_m (1 - 0.63\omega') = 0.0555(12)(5.25)^2(2{,}000)\left[1 - 0.63(0.0555)\right] \\ &= 35{,}430 \text{ in.-lb/ft} \\ &= 2{,}952 \text{ ft-lb/ft} \end{aligned}$$

$$\phi = 0.9 \quad \phi M_n = (0.9)(2{,}952) = 2{,}657 > 1{,}106 \text{ ft-lb} \qquad \text{OK}$$

Check interaction: $$\frac{P_u}{\phi P_n} + \frac{M_u}{\phi M_n} = \frac{2{,}750}{89{,}726} + \frac{1{,}106}{2{,}657} = 0.03 + 0.42 = 0.45 < 1.0$$

#5 @ 32 in., 8 in. CMU OK for loads.

601. **(Continued)**

(b) Footing bearing and stability

Overturning stability:

Footing wt = (3 ft)(1 ft)(150 lb/ft^3) = 450 plf
Total DL = 3,000 plf + 450 plf (footing wt) + 450 × 1.33 plf (soil wt) = 4,050 plf
Soil wt = (450 psf) (1.33 ft) = 600 plf
ΣP = 3,000 plf (DL) + 450 plf (FTG) + 600 plf (SOIL)
  = 4,050 plf

Overturning moment = 600 plf × 2.5 ft = 1,500 ft-lb/ft.

Calculate resisting moment about bottom of right corner of footing:

$$M_R = (3,000 \text{ plf})(1.33 \text{ ft}) + (450 \text{ plf})(1.5 \text{ ft}) + (600 \text{ plf})\left(3 \text{ ft} - \frac{1.333}{2}\text{ft}\right)$$

$$\Sigma M_{R_{D+SOIL}} = 6,075 \text{ ft-lb/ft}$$

$$\text{Factor of safety against overturning} = \frac{6,075}{1,500} = 4.05 > 1.5 \quad \text{OK}$$

Bearing:

$$e' = \frac{M}{P} = \frac{6,075 - 1,500}{4,050} = 1.13 \text{ ft} \qquad \left(\begin{array}{l}\text{eccentricity with respect to bottom right} \\ \text{corner of footing}\end{array}\right)$$

$$e = \frac{L_{footing}}{2} - e' = \frac{3 \text{ ft}}{2} - 1.13 \text{ ft} = 0.37 \text{ ft}$$

Resultant is within middle third of footing $(L/6 = 0.5 \text{ ft})$, i.e., inside of kern.

$$\therefore \ q_{max} = \frac{P\left(1 + \frac{6e}{L}\right)}{BL} = \frac{4,050\left(1 + \frac{6(0.37)}{3}\right)}{(1)(3)} = 2,349 \text{ psf}$$

q_{max} < allowable soil bearing pressure = 3,000 psf   OK

601. **(Continued)**

Sliding:

Sliding force = 600 plf (given)

Determine frictional resistance provided:

$\{3,000 \text{ plf} + 450 \text{ plf (footing)} + 600 \text{ plf (soil)}\} \times (\text{static friction coefficient} = 0.28) = 1,134 \text{ lb/ft}$

Determine passive pressure resistance provided:

$P_P = (K_P = 2.5) \times 110 \text{ pcf} = 275 \text{ psf/ft}$ (Assume provided P_P does not need to be reduced for soil mobilization.)

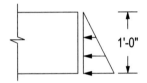

Resisting force provided = 275 psf/ft (1 ft)(1 ft)(1/2) = 138 plf

Sliding resistance = 1,134 + 138 = 1,272 plf

Factor of safety = 1,272/600 = 2.12 > 1.5   OK

601. (Continued)

(c) Wall-to-footing connection

Tension development length for 90° hook, $\ell_{dh} = \left(0.02\psi f_y /\lambda\sqrt{f'_c}\right) d_b$ ACI 318, Sec.12.5.2

$\psi = 1.0$ $\lambda = 1.0$

$f_y = 60,000$ $f'_c = 3,000$ $d_b = 5/8$ in.

$$\therefore \ell_{dh} = \left(\frac{(0.02)(60,000)}{\sqrt{3,000}}\right)\left(\frac{5}{8}\right)$$

$\quad\quad\quad = 13.7$ in. > 9 in.: try using reduction factors.

12.5.3 Reduction factor for No. 11 bar and smaller with side cover $> 2\ 1/2$ in. for 90° hook $= 0.7$

$\ell_{dh} = 13.7 \times 0.7 = 9.6$ in. > 9 in. try reduction factor for excess reinforcement

From solution for **Requirement (a).**

Assume moment applied/steel moment strength is proportional to A_s required/A_s provided.

$$\frac{M_a}{M_{steel}} = \frac{691}{1,507} = 0.46$$

$$\frac{M_u}{\phi M_n} = \frac{1,106}{2,657} = 0.42$$

$\ell_{dh} = 0.46 \times 9.6 = 4.4$ in. > 9 in.

OR $0.42 \times 9.6 = 4.0$ in. > 9 in.

However ℓ_{dh} not less than $8\ d_b$ or 6 in. $\therefore$ Use $\ell_{dh} = 6$ in.   ACI 318 Secction 12.5.1

Per ACI 318 Section 7.1.2, standard hook is $12\ d_b$ extension.

$12 \times \dfrac{5}{8}$ in. $= 7.5$ in.   use 8 in.

Connection of wall to footing:

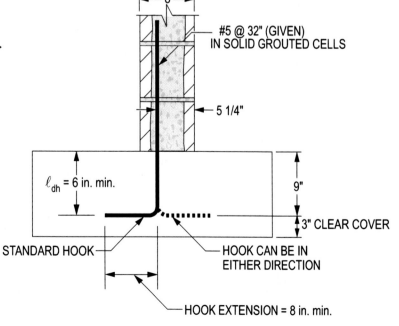

97

602. **(a)**   Service dead load =   850 plf
                     Service live load =   1,250 plf

Load combination 16–2 $1.2D + 1.6L$

$1.2 \times 850 + 1.6 \times 1,250 = 3,020 \text{ lb/ft}$

Since forces are for a unit load of 1,000 plf, all loads given in **Figure 602B** must be factored by a factor of $3,020/1,000 = 3.02$

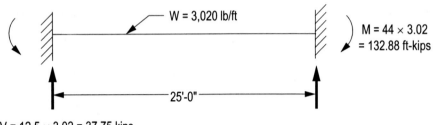

$V = 12.5 \times 3.02 = 37.75 \text{ kips}$

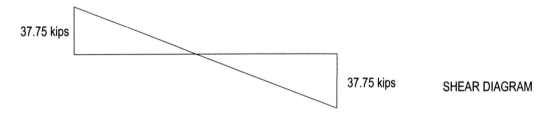

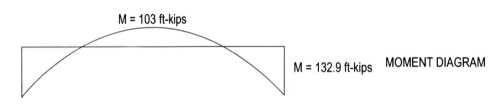

Moment at center span

$M = (1/2)(37.75 \text{ kips})(12.5 \text{ ft}) - 132.9 \text{ ft-kips} = 103 \text{ ft-kips}$

602. **(Continued)**

(b) Design of beam-column connection

Tension/compression force at beam flange:

W21 × 44   d = 20.7

$$\frac{M}{d} = \frac{132.9 \times 12}{20.7} = 77 \text{ kips}$$

$$\text{Top flange force} = 77 + \frac{(2.0)(3.02)}{2} = 80 \text{ kips}$$

$$\text{Bottom flange force} = 77 - \frac{(2.0)(3.02)}{2} = 74 \text{ kips}$$

Area of flange P_L required:

Flange P_L tension yielding: AISC Eq. D2-1

$$80 = \phi F_y A_g$$

$$A_g = \frac{80}{(0.9)(36)}$$

$$A_g \text{ required} = 2.47 \text{ in}^2$$

Try 3/8" × 6 3/4" P_L $A = 2.53 \text{ in}^2 > 2.47 \text{ in}^2$

Check net section:

Flange P_L tension rupture: AISC Eq. D2-2

$$\phi P_n = F_u A_e$$

$$A_e = U A_n \qquad U = 1.0$$ AISC Table D3-1 (Case 1)

(6) 3/4" A325N bolts at Flange P_L in 2 rows

$$A_n = \left[6.75 - 2\left(\frac{3}{4} + \frac{1}{16}\right) \right] \times \frac{3}{8} = 1.922 \text{ in}^2$$

$$\phi P_n = 0.75 \times 58 \times 1.922 = 83.6 \text{ kips} > 80 \text{ kips} \qquad \text{OK}$$

∴ Use flange P_L 3/8" × 6 3/4"

Check capacity of bolts in flange plate:

Per AISC Table 7.1:

Capacity of 3/4" dia. A325N bolts (Group A bolts) in single shear, $\phi r_n = 17.9$ kips
6 bolts × 17.9 kips = 107.4 kips > 80 kips   OK

602. (Continued)

Per AISC Table 7-4:

Check bearing strength based on 3 in. spacing of standard holes, $\phi r_n = 78.3$ kips/in. thickness

For 3/8 in. P_L, $78.3 \times 3/8 = 29.4$ kips > 17.9 ∴ Does not control

Per AISC Table 7-5:

Check bearing strength based on 2 in. edge spacing of standard holes, $\phi r_n = 78.3$ kips/in. thickne

For 3/8 in. P_L, $78.3 \times 3/8 = 29.4$ kips > 17.9 ∴ Does not control

Check weld required for flange P_L to column:

Fillet weld size required for E70XX

$$\phi R_n = \phi F_{nw} A_{we} \qquad\qquad \text{AISC Eq. J2.4}$$

$$\phi = 0.75$$

$$F_{nw} = 0.60\, F_{EXX} \left(1.0 + 0.50 \sin^{1.5} \theta\right)$$

$$= 0.60\,(70)\left(1.0 + 0.50 \sin^{1.5} 90\right) = 63 \text{ ksi}$$

$$A_{we} = t_e \ell$$

$$= 0.707\,(D/16)(6\ 3/4")(2)$$

$$= 0.597\,D$$

$$(0.75)(63)(0.597\,D) = 80 \text{ kips}$$

∴ $D = 2.8 \Rightarrow 3/16"$ fillet weld

However, AISC Table J2.4 requires min. 1/4" fillet weld for 3/4" thick material

∴ Use 1/4" fillet weld top and bottom of flange P_L

For single shear P_L web connection to column:

Try a P_L 3/8" × 4" × 9" with (3) 3/4" dia. A325N bolts (Group A bolts)

Per AISC Table 10-10a, LRFD available strengths = 43.4 kips > 37.8 kips   OK

602. **(Continued)**

Check if stiffeners are required in column:

Local flange bending: AISC, Sec. J10.1

$$R_n = 6.25\, t_f^2 F_{yf} \qquad t_f = 0.72" \text{ for W14} \times 68$$

$$R_n = 6.25 \times 0.72^2 \times 50 = 162 \text{ kips}$$

$$\phi R_n = 146 \text{ kips since } \phi = 0.9 > 80 \text{ kips} \qquad \text{OK}$$

Web local yielding:

$$R_n = (5k + \ell_b) F_{yw}\, t_w \text{ For W14} \times 68, \text{ k} = 1.31, t_w = 0.415, \ell_b = 0.375 \quad \text{AISC, Eq. J10-2}$$

$$R_n = (5 \times 1.31 + 0.375) \times 50 \times 0.415 = 143 \text{ kips}$$

$$\phi R_n = 143 \text{ kips for } \phi = 1.0 > 80 \text{ kips} \qquad \text{OK}$$

Web local crippling:

$$R_n = 0.8\, t_w^2 \left[1 + 3\left(\frac{\ell_b}{d} \right)\left(\frac{t_w}{t_f} \right)^{1.5} \right] \times \sqrt{\frac{E \times F_{yw} \times t_f}{t_w}} \qquad \text{AISC, Eq. J10-4}$$

$$t_w = 0.415 \qquad \ell_b = 0.375 \qquad d = 14 \text{ in.} \qquad t_f = 0.72$$

$$R_n = 0.8\left(0.415^2\right)\left[1 + 3\left(\frac{0.375}{14} \right)\left(\frac{0.415}{0.72} \right)^{1.5} \right] \times \sqrt{\frac{29 \times 10^3 \times 50 \times 0.72}{0.415}}$$

$$R_n = 226 \text{ kips}$$

$$\phi R_n = 169 \text{ kips since } \phi = 0.75 \text{ kips} > 74 \text{ kips} \qquad \text{OK}$$

No web stiffeners are required.

602. (Continued)

(c) Sketch of connection detail

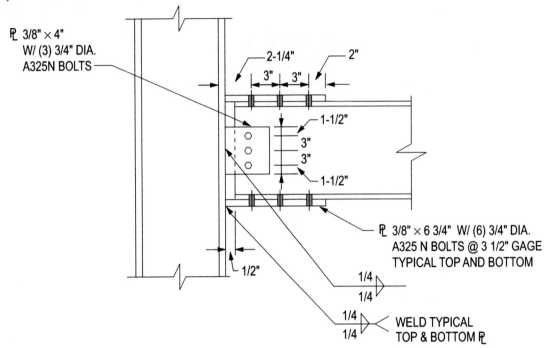

℄ 3/8" × 4"
W/ (3) 3/4" DIA.
A325N BOLTS

2-1/4"
2"
3"
3"

1-1/2"
3"
3"
1-1/2"

1/2"

℄ 3/8" × 6 3/4" W/ (6) 3/4" DIA.
A325 N BOLTS @ 3 1/2" GAGE
TYPICAL TOP AND BOTTOM

1/4
1/4

1/4
1/4

WELD TYPICAL
TOP & BOTTOM ℄

603. **(a) Determine maximum factored shear and moment in floor beam**

Calculate factored loads at beam at floor:

Floor DL $= 130$ psf $\times 30$ ft $= 3{,}900$ plf

Floor LL $= 70$ psf

Per ASCE-7 Section 4.7.2 or IBC Section 1607.10.1:

$$L = L_0\left(0.25 + \frac{15}{\sqrt{K_u A_T}}\right)$$

$$= 70\left(0.25 + \frac{15}{\sqrt{2 \times 30 \times 30}}\right) = 70(0.60) = 42 \text{ psf}$$

Floor LL $= 42$ psf $\times 30$ ft $= 1{,}260$ plf

$U = 1.2\,D + 1.6\,L$ \hfill IBC Eq. 16-2

$= 1.2(3.9) + 1.6(1.26)$

$= 4.68 + 2.02 = 6.70$ kips/ft

Calculate moments and shears: \hfill ACI Section 8.3.3

Clear span beam 3-4

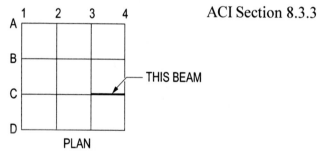

$\ell_n = 30.0 - 2.0 - \dfrac{2.0}{2} = 27.0$ ft

Clear span beam 2-4

$\ell_n = 30.0 - \dfrac{2.0}{2} - \dfrac{2.0}{2} = 28.0$ ft

End span $M^+ = \dfrac{w_u \ell_n^2}{14}$ (discontinuous end integral with support)

$$= \frac{6.7 \times 27^2}{14} = 349 \text{ ft-kips}$$

M^- at exterior face of first interior support $= \dfrac{w_u \ell_n^2}{10}$ (more than two spans)

$\ell_n = \dfrac{27 + 28}{2} = 27.5$

$M^- = \dfrac{6.7 \times 27.5^2}{10} = 507$ ft-kips

M^- at exterior face at exterior column $= \dfrac{w_u \ell_n^2}{16} = \dfrac{6.7 \times 27^2}{16} = 305$ ft-kips

Shear in end member at face of first interior support $\quad 1.15\, w_u \ell_n/2 = (1.15)(6.7)(27/2) = 104.0$ kips

Shear at face of all other supports $\qquad w_u \ell_n/2 \qquad = 6.7 \times 27/2 = 90.5$ kips

603. **(Continued)**

(b) Sketch the shear and moment diagrams for the beam in Requirement (a).

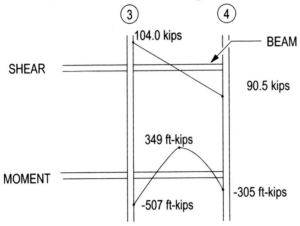

SHEAR AND MOMENT DIAGRAMS

(c) Design the beam for maximum positive moment in the span and negative moment and shear at column grid.

Positive moment (design as T-beam):

$M_u = 349$ ft-kips

Effective flange width :

$\text{span}/4 = \dfrac{27}{4}$ ft $\times$ 12 in./ft $= 81$ in. (controls)

or $18" + 8(9")(2) = 162$ in.

or $18" + \dfrac{27}{2} \times 12$ in./ft $= 180$ in.

$d = 24 - (1.5 + 0.5 + 0.5) = 21.5$ in.

From design aids:

$M_u / \phi bd^2 = \dfrac{349 \times 12,000}{0.9 \times 81 \times 21.5^2} = 124.3$

(Note: since the thickness of the slab flanges > a, design as rectangular section with tension reinforcing only)

From the table, $\rho = 0.0022$

$A_s = \rho bd = 0.0022 \times 81 \times 21.5 = 3.83$ in^2

Min steel $A_{s\,min} = 3\sqrt{f'_c}\, b_w d/f_y = \dfrac{3\sqrt{4,000} \times 18 \times 21.5}{60,000}$ ACI 318 Sec. 10.5

$= 1.22$ in$^2 < 200\, b_w d/f_y = \dfrac{200 \times 18 \times 21.5}{60,000} = 1.29$ in^2

$\therefore A_{s\,required} = 3.83$ in^2 Use (5) #8 bars

603. (Continued)

Negative moment at exterior face of first interior column:

$$M_u = 507 \text{ ft-kips} \qquad b = 18 \text{ in.} \qquad d = 21.5 \text{ in.}$$

$$\frac{M_u}{\phi bd^2} = \frac{507 \times 12,000}{0.9 \times 18 \times 21.5^2} = 812.5$$

From the table, $\rho = 0.0158$

Area of steel $= 0.0158 \times 18 \times 21.5 = 6.12 \text{ in}^2$

$$\text{Min steel } A_{s \, min} = 3\sqrt{f'_c}\, b_w d/f_y = \frac{3\sqrt{4,000} \times 18 \times 21.5}{60,000}$$

$$= 1.22 \text{ in}^2 < 200 \, b_w d/f_y = \frac{200 \times 18 \times 21.5}{60,000} = 1.29 \text{ in}^2$$

$$\therefore A_{s \, required} = 6.12 \text{ in}^2 \qquad \text{Use (5) #10 bars}$$

Shear:

$$V_u = 104.0 \text{ kips}$$

$$1/2\,\phi V_c = \phi 2bd\sqrt{f'_c} = \frac{0.75 \times 2 \times 18 \times 21.5 \times \sqrt{4,000}}{(2)(1,000)} = 18.4 < 104.0; \text{ Shear steel req.}$$

Use #4; $A_v = 2 \times 0.2 = 0.4 \text{ in}^2$

$$\text{Spacing } s = \frac{A_v f_{yt} d}{V_s/\phi} = \frac{0.4 \times 60 \times 21.5}{\left(\dfrac{104.0 - 18.4(2)}{0.75}\right)} = 5.76 \text{ in. Use 5 in.}$$

Maximum spacing to provide minimum A_v:

$$s = \frac{A_v f_y}{0.75 \times \sqrt{f'_c}\, b_w} = \frac{(0.4)(60,000)}{0.75 \times \sqrt{4,000}\,(18)} = 28.1 \text{ in.}$$

$$s = \frac{A_v f_y}{50\, b_w} = \frac{(0.4)(60,000)}{50(18)} = 26.7 \text{ in.}$$

$$4\sqrt{f'_c}\, b_w d = \frac{4\sqrt{4,000}\,(18)(21.5)}{1,000} = 97.9 \text{ kips}$$

$$V_s = \frac{104.0 - (2)(18.4)}{0.75} = 49.1 \text{ kips} < 97.9 \text{ kips}$$

$$\therefore \text{Max } s = \frac{d}{2} = \frac{21.5}{2} = 10.75 \text{ in.}$$

$$\therefore \text{Use #4 stirrups @ 5 in. o.c.}$$

603.   (Continued)

(d) Show all of the beam reinforcing at Joint 1 and column steel.

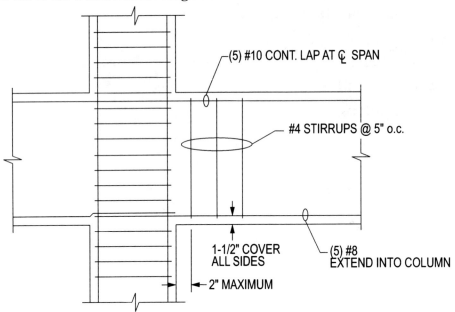

604. **(a) Determine the forces in each of the truss members.**

Consider the loading conditions after demolition and with new equipment load.

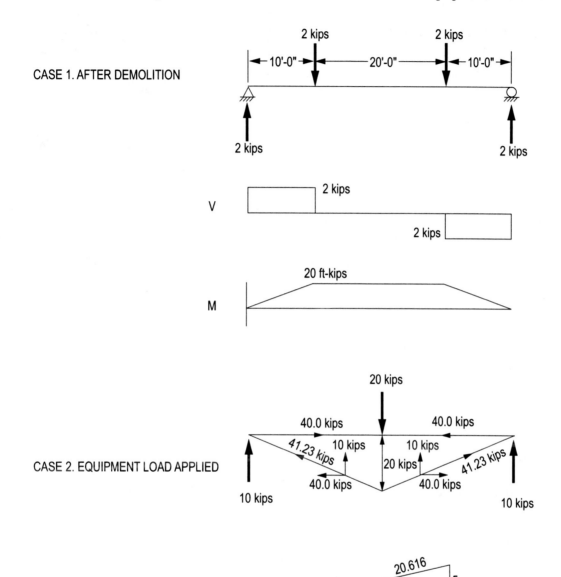

604. (Continued)

(b) Glulam 8 1/2 × 26 1/8 SP

From NDS Supplement Table 10:

$A = 222.1 \text{ in}^2$

$I_x = 12{,}630 \text{ in}^4$

$S_x = 966.9 \text{ in}^3$

$r_x = 7.542 \text{ in.}$

From Table 604A:

$F_{b^+_{x(\text{tension zone in tension})}}$	2,400 psi
$F_{b^-_{x(\text{compression zone in tension})}}$	1,450 psi
$F_{c_{\perp x}}$	500 psi
F_{v_x}	210 psi
F_t	775 psi
F_c	1,000 psi
E_x	1.7×10^6 psi
E_{axial}	1.37×10^6 psi
$E_{x_{min}}$	0.9×10^6 psi
E_y	1.3×10^6 psi
$E_{y_{min}}$	0.69×10^6 psi
G	0.55

$C_D = 0.90, C_M = C_t = 1.0$

$$C_V = \left(\frac{21}{L}\right)^{1/x}\left(\frac{12}{d}\right)^{1/x}\left(\frac{5.125}{b}\right)^{1/x} < 1.0 \qquad \text{NDS Eq. 5.3-1}$$

$x = 20$ for Southern Pine

$L = 40$ ft

$$C_V = \left(\frac{21}{40}\right)^{1/20}\left(\frac{12}{26.125}\right)^{1/20}\left(\frac{5.125}{8.5}\right)^{1/20} = 0.908 < 1.0$$

Existing glulam girder flexure:

Tension laminations in tension

$$F'_{bx} = 2{,}400 \times C_D \times C_V = 2{,}400 \times 0.9 \times 0.908 = 1{,}961 \text{ psi}$$

Maximum moment = 20 ft-kips

$$f_{b\ \text{tension side}} = \frac{M}{S_x} = \frac{20 \text{ ft-kips} \times 12 \times 1{,}000}{966.9 \text{ in}^3} = 248 \text{ psi} < 1{,}961 \text{ psi} \qquad \text{OK}$$

604. **(Continued)**

Existing glulam girder compression:

$$\left(\frac{\ell_e}{d}\right)_x = \frac{(1.0)(40\,\text{ft})(12)}{26.125} = 18.4$$

$$\left(\frac{\ell_e}{d}\right)_y = \frac{(1.0)(20\,\text{ft})(12)}{8.5} = 28.2 \Leftarrow \text{Controls}$$

$$E_{y\,\text{min}} = 0.69 \times 10^6 \,\text{psi} = E'_{\text{min}}$$

$$C_p = \frac{1 + F_{cE}/F_c^*}{2c} - \sqrt{\left[\frac{1 + F_{cE}/F_c^*}{2\,c}\right]^2 - \frac{F_{cE}/F_c^*}{c}} \qquad\qquad \text{NDS Eq. 3.7}-1$$

$$F_{cE} = \frac{0.822\,E'_{\text{min}}}{(\ell_e/d)^2} \qquad\qquad \text{NDS Sec. 3.7.1}$$

$$F_{cE} = \frac{0.822\left(0.69 \times 10^6\right)}{(28.2)^2} = 713\,\text{psi}$$

$$F_c^* = 1{,}000(0.9) = 900\,\text{psi}$$

$$c = 0.9 \text{ for glulams}$$

$$\therefore C_p = 0.66$$

$$F'_c = 1{,}000 \times C_D \times C_p = 1{,}000 \times 0.9 \times 0.66 = 594\,\text{psi}$$

Maximum compression = 40 kips

$$f_c = \frac{P}{A} = \frac{40 \times 1{,}000}{222.1} = 180\,\text{psi} \qquad \text{OK}$$

Existing glulam girder combined stress:

$$\left[\frac{f_c}{F'_c}\right]^2 + \frac{f_{b1}}{F'_{b1}\left[1 - \left(f_c/F_{cE1}\right)\right]} \leq 1.0 \qquad\qquad \text{NDS Eq. 3.9}-3$$

$$F_{cE1} = \frac{0.822\,E'_{\text{min}}}{(\ell_{e1}/d_1)^2} = \frac{0.822\left(0.9 \times 10^6\right)}{(18.4)^2} = 2{,}185\,\text{psi}$$

$$\left[\frac{180}{594}\right]^2 + \frac{248}{1{,}961\left[1 - \left(180/2{,}185\right)\right]} = 0.23 < 1.0 \qquad \text{OK}$$

604. (Continued)

(c) Truss rod end connection

$Z_{\parallel} = 3,480 \text{ lb}$ NDS Table 11-I

$Z_{\perp} = 2,000 \text{ lb}$

$\theta = 14° \qquad \sin\theta = 0.242 \qquad \cos\theta = 0.970$

$C_D = 0.9 \qquad C_g = 0.95 \text{ (given) } C_\Delta = 1.0$

$$Z_\theta = \frac{Z_{\parallel}Z_{\perp}}{Z_{\parallel}\sin^2\theta + Z_{\perp}\cos^2\theta} = \frac{(3,480)(2,000)}{(3,480)(0.0585)+(2,000)(0.9415)}$$

$$= \frac{6,960,000}{203.6+1,883.0} = 3,336 \text{ lb}$$

$Z_\phi' = C_d C_g Z_\phi = (0.9)(0.95)(3,336) = 2,852 \text{ lb}$

For (10) 3/4" dia. bolts 10(2,852 lb) = 28,520 lb

28.520 kips < 35 kips

∴ New bolts at new tension rod connection are not adequate.

VERTICAL FORCES PM BRIDGES SOLUTIONS

701. **(a) Determine flexural strength for Strength I Limit State at midspan. Check minimum steel.**

A_{ps} = (34 strands) (0.153 in^2/strand) = 5.20 in^2

$f_{ps} = f_{pu}\left(1 - k\dfrac{c}{d_p}\right)$

Eq. 5.7.3.1.1-1

$k = 2\left(1.04 - \dfrac{f_{py}}{f_{pu}}\right)$

Eq. 5.7.3.1.1-2

$f_{pu} = 270$ ksi

$\beta_1 = 0.85$

Art. 5.7.2.2

$f_{py} = 0.9\, f_{pu}$

Table 5.4.4.1-1

Determine d_p:

$\bar{x}\ @\ \mathcal{C} = \dfrac{12\times2.5 + 12\times4.5 + 6\times6.5 + 2\times8.5 + 2\times10.5}{34} = 4.74$ in.

$d_p\ @\ \mathcal{C} = 70.5 - 4.74 = 65.76$ in.

$k = 2(1.04 - 0.90) = 0.28$

Assume rectangular section behavior.

$c = 5.20\text{ in}^2\,(270\text{ ksi})/\left[(0.85)(4\text{ ksi})(0.85)(66) + 0.28(5.20\text{ in}^2)\left(\dfrac{270\text{ ksi}}{65.76}\right)\right]$

$= 7.14$ in. < 7.50 in.   OK

Eq. 5.7.3.1.1-4

$f_{ps} = f_{pu}\left(1 - k\dfrac{c}{d_p}\right) = 270\left(1 - (0.28)\dfrac{7.14}{65.76}\right) = 261.8$ ksi

Eq. 5.7.3.1.1-1

$a = 0.85(7.14) = 6.07$ in.

Art. 5.7.2.2

$M_n = A_{ps}f_{ps}\left(d_p - \dfrac{a}{2}\right)$

Art. 5.7.3.2.3
Eq. 5.7.3.2.2-1

$M_n = 5.20\text{ in}^2\,(261.8\text{ ksi})\left(65.76 - \dfrac{6.07}{2}\right)\dfrac{1}{12} = 7{,}116$ ft-kips

$\phi = 1.0$ Assume tension-controlled p/s concrete

Art 5.5.4.2.1

Verify tension-controlled assumption.

$\dfrac{0.003}{c} = \dfrac{E_S}{d-c}$

$\dfrac{0.003(d-c)}{c} = E_S$

$\dfrac{0.003(65.76\text{ in.} - 7.14\text{ in.})}{7.14\text{ in.}} = 0.025 > 0.005$

Tension-controlled, $\phi = 1.0$

112

701. **(Continued)**

DC moment:

$$(1.3 \text{ kips}/\text{ft}) \frac{(120^2)}{8} = 2,340 \text{ ft-kips}$$

DW moment:

$$(0.26 \text{ kips}/\text{ft}) \frac{(120)^2}{8} = 468 \text{ ft-kips}$$

LL+ IM = 1,830 ft-kips

Strength I   Tables 3.4.1-1

M_u = 1.25 DC + 1.50 DW + 1.75 (LL+IM)   3.4.1-2

    = 1.25 (2,340 ft-kips) + 1.50 (468 ft-kips) + 1.75 (1,830 ft-kips)

    = 6,830 ft-kips < (1.0) (7,116 ft-kips)   OK

Check minimum steel: Art. 5.7.3.3.2

$\phi M_n > M_{cr}$

$$M_{cr} = \gamma_3 \left[\left(\gamma_1 f_r + \gamma_2 f_{cpe} \right) S_c + M_{dnc} \left(\frac{S_c}{S_{nc}} - 1 \right) \right]$$ Eq. 5.7.3.3.2-1

$f_r = 0.24 \sqrt{f'_c}$

    $= 0.24 \left(\sqrt{6} \right) = 0.59 \text{ ksi}$

$\gamma_1 = 1.2$ Art. 5.4.2.6

$\gamma_2 = 1.1$

$\gamma_3 = 1.00$

S_c = 15,767 in^3 S @ bottom of composite section

S_{ncb} = 12,224 in^3 S @ bottom of precast section

M_{dnc} = 2,340 ft-kips   Noncomposite DC moment

$$f_{pe} = \frac{\text{prestress}}{A} + \frac{(\text{prestress})(e)(c)}{I}$$

Prestress = P_{jack} − losses

    = (0.75)(270 ksi) − 40.5 ksi

    = 162 ksi

Prestress force = (162 ksi)(5.202 in^2) = 843 kips

e = 32.12 − 4.74 = 27.38 in.

701. (Continued)

$$f_{cpe} = \frac{843 \text{ kips}}{713 \text{ in}^2} + \frac{(843 \text{ kips})(27.38 \text{ in.})(32.12 \text{ in.})}{392,638 \text{ in}^4} = 3.07 \text{ ksi}$$

$$M_{cr} = 1.0\left[\left((1.2)(0.59 \text{ ksi}) + (1.1)(3.07 \text{ ksi})\right)(15,767 \text{ in}^4) - 2,340 \text{ ft-kips}\left(\frac{12 \text{ in.}}{\text{ft}}\right)\left(\frac{15,767 \text{ in}^4}{12,224 \text{ in}^4} - 1\right)\right]$$

$$= 56,269 \text{ in.-kips}$$

$$= 4,689 \text{ ft-kips} < 7,119 \text{ ft-kips} \qquad \therefore \text{ minimums do not control}$$

$$\text{Section is adequate} \leftarrow \text{(a)}$$

(b) Determine and sketch anchorage zone vertical reinforcing for the girder using #5 bars.

AASHTO 5.10.10.1 covers pretensioned anchorage.

Prestress force is *before* losses, at P initial transfer

Prestress force = (270 ksi)(0.75)(0.153 in.^{2})(34 strands) = 1,053 kips

4% of this force = 0.04(1,053 kips) = 42.12 kips

$$A_s \text{ required acting @ 20 ksi} = \frac{42.12 \text{ kips}}{20 \text{ ksi}} = 2.106 \text{ in}^2$$

$$\text{Number of #5 bars} = \frac{2.106 \text{ in}^2}{0.31 \text{ in}^2} = 6.79 \approx 8 \text{ bars or 4 stirrups} \quad \sqcup$$

Place these bars within h/4 of the end of the beam

h @ end of the beam is 63 in.

$$\frac{h}{4} = \frac{63}{4} = 15.75 \text{ in.} \qquad \text{Use 4 #5 stirrups @ 4 in. spacing}$$

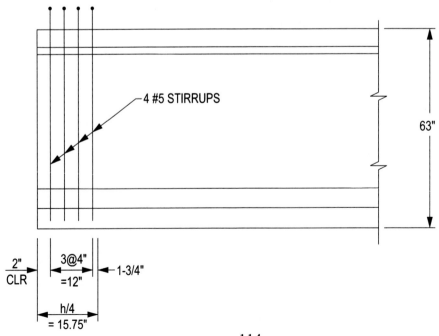

114

702. **(a) Determine dead load moment for Girder A.**

$W_{girder} = 0.50$ klf (given)

$$W_{deck} = \left[\left(\frac{7' - 6"}{2} + 3' - 9"\right)\right]\left(\frac{8 \text{ in.}}{(12 \text{ in./ft})}\right)(0.150 \text{ kcf}) = 0.75 \text{ kip/ft}$$

$$W_{barrier} = \frac{2 \text{ barriers}}{4 \text{ girders}}\left[(2'-6")(1 \text{ ft})\right](0.150 \text{ kcf}) = 0.19 \text{ kip/ft}$$

$$W_{DC} = 0.50 + 0.75 + 0.19 = 1.44 \text{ kips/ft}$$

$$M_{DC} = \frac{wL^2}{8} = \frac{(1.44 \text{ kips/ft})(120 \text{ ft})^2}{8} = 2{,}592 \text{ ft-kips}$$

Determine wearing surface moment for Girder A.

$$W_{DW} = \frac{[30'- 2(1'-0")]}{4 \text{ girders}}\left(\frac{2 \text{ in.}}{12 \text{ in./ft}}\right)(0.140 \text{ kcf}) = 0.163 \text{ kip/ft} \qquad \text{Table 3.5-1-1}$$

$$M_{DW} = \frac{wL^2}{8} = \frac{(0.163 \text{ kips/ft})(120 \text{ ft})^2}{8} = 293 \text{ ft-kips}$$

(b) Determine live load moment (HL-93) per lane. $\qquad$ Art. 3.6.1.2.2

Design Truck

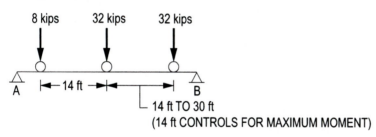

Note: It is sufficiently accurate to place the center axle at midspan.

$$\Sigma M_B = 0 = -(32 \text{ kips})(60' - 14') - (32 \text{ kips})(60') - (8 \text{ kips})(60'+ 14') + R_A(120')$$

$$R_A = \frac{(32 \text{ kips})(46') + (32 \text{ kips})(60') + (8 \text{ kips})(74')}{120'} = \frac{3{,}984 \text{ ft-kips}}{120'} = 33.2 \text{ kips}$$

$$\Sigma M_{\mathbb{C}} = 0 = (33.2 \text{ kips})(60') - (8 \text{ kips})(14') - M_{truck} = 0$$

$$M_{truck/lane} = 1{,}880 \text{ ft-kips/lane}$$

702. (Continued)

Design tandem

Note: Ignore design tandem (given)

Design lane

$W_{lane} = 0.64 \text{ klf } \left(\text{over } 10' \text{ width}\right)$ Art. 3.6.1.2.4

$$M_{lane/lane} = \frac{wL^2}{8} = \frac{0.64 \text{ klf }(120')^2}{8} = 1,152 \text{ ft-kips}$$

Dynamic Load Allowance (IM)

Strength I limit state for girder => IM = 33%   Art. 3.6.2

$$IM_{factor \text{ for truck}} = \left(1 + \frac{33}{100}\right) = 1.33$$

Application of design vehicular live loads.   Art. 3.6.1.3

    Combine design truck with dynamic load allowance and lane load

    Design lane placed to produce extreme force

    Outside wheel of design truck placed 2' - 0" from edge of design lane for girders

$$M_{LL + IM/lane} = 1,880 \text{ ft-kips } (1.33) + 1,152 \text{ ft-kips} = 3,652 \text{ ft-kips/lane}$$

(c) Determine distribution of live loads per lane for moments in exterior longitudinal beams.

Typical cross section (k)   Table 4.6.2.2.1-1

L = 120' - 0"   Table C4.6.2.2.1-1

One lane loaded: Lever rule   Table 4.6.2.2.2d-1

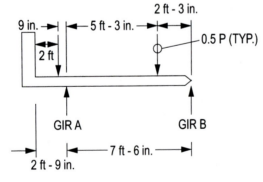

$$\Sigma M_B = 0 = -0.5P(2.25') - 0.5P(6' + 2.25') + DF_{ext}(7.5')$$

$$g_{ext \text{ lever}} = \frac{1.125P + 4.125P}{7.5'}$$

With P = 1.0

$g_{ext \text{ lever}} = 0.700$

m = 1.20   Table 3.6.1.1.2-1

g = 0.700(1.20) = 0.840

702. **(Continued)**

Two or more design lanes loaded

$g = e \, g_{interior}$ erior \hfill Table 4.6.2.2.2d-1

$e = 0.77 + \dfrac{d_e}{9.1}$ \hfill Table 4.6.2.2.2d

d_e is taken as positive if $\mathcal{C}$ girder is inboard of face of curb

$d_e = (3\text{'-}9") - (1\text{'-}0") = 2\text{'-}9"$

Application $-1.0 \le d_e = 2.75 \le 5.5$

$e = 0.77 + \dfrac{d_e}{9.1}$

$e = 0.77 + \left(\dfrac{2.75}{9.1}\right) = 1.072$

Given: $\quad f_c'$ (girder) $= 7.0$ ksi $\qquad W_{girder} = 0.150$ kcf

$\qquad\qquad f_c'$ (C.I.P.) $= 4.0$ ksi $\qquad W_{C.I.P.} = 0.150$ kcf

$E_{girder} = 33{,}000 \, K_1 \, W_c^{1.5} \sqrt{f_c'} = 33{,}000(1.0)(0.150)^{1.5}\sqrt{7.0} = 5{,}072$ ksi \hfill Eq. 5.4.2.4-1

$E_{C.I.P.} = 33{,}000(1.0)(0.150)^{1.5}\sqrt{4.0} = 3{,}834$ ksi

$n = \dfrac{E_B}{E_D} = \dfrac{5{,}072}{3{,}834} = 1.32$ \hfill Eq. 4.6.2.2.1-2

$K_g = n\left(I + A e_g^2\right)$ \hfill Eq. 4.6.2.2.1-1

$\quad = 1.32\left[265{,}320 + 570(28)^2\right] = 940{,}104 \text{ in}^4$

One design lane loaded: $g_{int} = 0.06 + \left(\dfrac{s}{14}\right)^{0.4}\left(\dfrac{s}{L}\right)^{0.3}\left(\dfrac{K_g}{12.0 \, L \, t_s^3}\right)^{0.1}$ \hfill Table 4.6.2.2.2b-1

Two or more design lanes loaded: $g_{int} = 0.075 + \left(\dfrac{s}{9.5}\right)^{0.6}\left(\dfrac{s}{L}\right)^{0.2}\left(\dfrac{K_g}{12.0 \, L \, t_s^3}\right)^{0.1}$

Applicability check:

$3.5 \le S = 7.5' \le 16.0 \quad$ OK $\qquad N_b = 4 \qquad$ OK
$4.5 \le t_s = 8" \le 12.0 \quad$ OK $\qquad 10{,}000 \le K_g = 940{,}104 \text{ in}^4 \le 7{,}000{,}000 \quad$ OK
$20 \le L = 120' \le 240 \quad$ OK

702. (Continued)

$$g_{int} = 0.06 + \left(\frac{7.5}{14}\right)^{0.4} \left(\frac{7.5}{120}\right)^{0.3} \left(\frac{940,104}{12.0(120)(8)^3}\right)^{0.1} = 0.408 \text{ one lane}$$

$$g_{int} = 0.075 + \left(\frac{7.5}{9.5}\right)^{0.6} \left(\frac{7.5}{120}\right)^{0.2} \left(\frac{940,104}{12.0(120)(8)^3}\right)^{0.1} = 0.586 \text{ two lanes}$$

$$g_{ext} = 1.072 (0.586) = 0.628$$

$$g_{ext} \text{ (controlling)} = \max[0.628, 0.840] = 0.840$$

(d) Determine factored load for Strength I limit state at midspan of Girder A.

Limit states Eq. 1.3.2.1-1 $\qquad \sum \eta_i \gamma_i Q_i \leq \phi R_n = R_r$ $\qquad\qquad$ Eq. 1.3.2.1-1

$\eta_i = \eta_D \eta_R \eta_I \geq 0.95$ maximum values $\qquad\qquad\qquad\qquad\qquad$ Eq. 1.3.2.1-2

For strength limit states

Ductility	$\eta_D = 1.0$	conventional design (given)	Art. 1.3.3
Redundancy	$\eta_R = 1.0$	conventionally redundant (given)	Art. 1.3.4
Operational importance	$\eta_I = 1.05$	important structure (given)	Art. 1.3.5

$\eta_i = (1.0)(1.0)(1.05) = 1.05 \geq 0.95$

$\gamma_{DC} = 1.25$ Max. $\qquad \gamma_{DW} = 1.50$ Max. $\qquad\qquad\qquad$ Tables 3.4.1-1 and 3.4.1-2

For Strength I Limit State

$$\sum \eta_i \gamma_i Q_i = \eta_I [\gamma_P (DC + DW) + 1.75 (LL + IM)]$$

$$M_u = (1.05)\left[1.25(2,592 \text{ ft-kips}) + 1.50 (293 \text{ ft-kips}) + 1.75(0.840)(3,652 \text{ ft-kips})\right]$$

$$= (1.05)\left[3,240 \text{ ft-kips} + 440 \text{ ft-kips} + 5,368 \text{ ft-kips}\right]$$

$$= 9,500 \text{ ft-kips at midspan of Girder A}$$

118

703. **(a) Verify the plate size for the flange splice.**

Per AASHTO Section 6.13.2.1, the connection must be checked for slip resistance and the shear and bearing resistance checked separately.

Calculate effective flange area—tension flange:

$$A_e = \left(\frac{\phi_u F_u}{\phi_y F_{yt}}\right) A_n$$ Eq. 6.13.6.1.4c-2

Deducted flange width for bolt hole = bolt diameter + 1/8 = 7/8 + 1/8 = 1 in.   Art. 6.8.3

$$
\begin{aligned}
W_n &= 16.5 - (4)(1) + (2)(3.5)^2/[(4)(3.5)] \\
&= 14.25 \text{ in.} \\
A_n &= (14.25)(1.26) \\
&= 17.96 \text{ in}^2 \\
A_g &= b_f \times t_f \\
&= (16.5)(1.26) \\
&= 20.79 \text{ in}^2
\end{aligned}
$$

$\phi_u = 0.80$ Art. 6.5.4.2

$\phi_y = 0.95$

$F_u = 58$ Table 6.4.1-1

$F_{yt} = 36$

$$A_e = \frac{(0.8)(58)}{(0.95)(36)}\left(17.96 \text{ in}^2\right)$$

$$= (1.357)\left(17.96 \text{ in}^2\right) = 24.37 \text{ in}^2 > A_g = 20.79 \text{ in}^2 \text{ Governs.}$$

The gross section properties can be used.

Determine the controlling flange:

Check each flange for stress at the midpoint of the flange due to tension forces from applied loads.

At the bottom flange (Dead Load + Maximum Positive Live Load):

Tables 3.4.1-1 & 2

$$
\begin{aligned}
M &= 0.9 \text{ DC} + 1.5 \text{ DW} + 1.75 \text{ (LL + I)} \\
&= 0.9(-69) + 1.5(26) + 1.75(730) \\
&= 1,254.4 \text{ ft-kips}
\end{aligned}
$$

$$
\begin{aligned}
S_x &= I_x/C \quad \text{At } \textbf{center} \text{ of beam flange} \\
&= 15,600/[(36.5 - 1.26)/2] \\
&= 885 \text{ in}^3
\end{aligned}
$$

703. **(Continued)**

$$f = M/S_X$$
$$= (1,254.4)(12)/885$$
$$= 17.01 \text{ ksi} \qquad \text{Controlling tension flange}$$

At the top flange (Dead Load + Maximum Negative Live Load):

$$M = 1.25(-69) + 1.75(-374) \text{ +0} \times DW$$
$$= 740.8 \text{ ft-kips}$$

The DW moment is conservatively omitted in this calculation.

$$S_X = I_X/C$$
$$= 15,600/[(36.5 - 1.26)/2]$$
$$= 885 \text{ in}^3$$

$$f = M/S_X$$
$$= (740.8)(12)/885$$
$$= 10.04 \text{ ksi} \qquad \text{Does not control}$$

Calculate design flange stresses:

Since the steel section is not composite with the concrete deck and the steel section is symmetric, the stress in both flanges is numerically the same under the controlling moment at the splices. Per AASHTO specs, both flanges must therefore be considered as the controlling flange because the absolute value of the stress ratio is the same. This means that the connection must be symmetric. Because stress reversal is possible, the flanges must also be checked for both loading cases. Since we are looking for the maximum stress condition in order to verify the connection, the flange with the maximum tension will be called the controlling flange while the other flange will be called the non-controlling flange (compressive stresses).

$$f_{cf} = 17.01 \text{ ksi (bottom flange controls)}$$

$$f_{ncf} = 17.01 \text{ ksi (compression)}$$

$$F_{cf} = (|f_{cf}/R_h| + \alpha\phi_f F_{yf})/2 \geq 0.75\,\alpha\phi_f F_{yf} \qquad \text{Eq. 6.13.6.1.4c-1}$$

$$\phi_f = 1.0 \qquad \text{Art. 6.5.4.2}$$

$$R_h = 1.0 \qquad \text{homogenous girder}$$

$$\alpha = 1.0$$

$$F_{yf} = 36 \text{ ksi} \qquad \text{Table 6.4.1-1}$$

$$0.75\alpha\phi_f F_{yf} = 27 \text{ ksi} \quad \text{minimum design flange yield stress}$$

$$F_{cf} = [|17.01/1.0| + (1.0)(36)]/2 = 26.51 \text{ ksi} < 27 \text{ ksi} \qquad \text{minimum controls}$$

$$F_{cf} = 27 \text{ ksi}$$

703. **(Continued)**

$$F_{ncf} = R_{cf} \, |f_{ncf}/R_h| \geq 0.75 \, \phi_f \alpha F_{yf} \qquad \text{Eq. 6.13.6.1.4c-3}$$

$$R_{cf} = |F_{cf}/f_{cf}|$$
$$= |27/17.01|$$
$$= 1.587$$

$$\alpha = 1.0$$

$$\phi_f = 1.00$$

$$F_{yf} = 36 \text{ ksi} \qquad\qquad\qquad \text{Table 6.4.1-1}$$

$$0.75\phi_f\alpha F_{yf} = 27 \text{ ksi} \qquad \text{minimum design flange yield stress}$$

$$F_{ncf} = (1.587)(|-17.01/1.0|) = 27 \text{ ksi} = 0.75 \, \alpha F_{yf} \qquad \text{so minimum controls}$$

$$F_{ncf} = 27 \text{ ksi}$$

Calculate design flange forces:

Tension flange force:
$$P_{cf} = F_{cf} \times A_e$$
$$= (27)(20.79)$$
$$= 561.3 \text{ kips}$$

Compression flange force:
For compression flanges, A_e always equals A_g

$$P_{ncf} = F_{ncf} \times A_e \quad \longrightarrow \boxed{\text{Effective flange area}}$$
$$= (27)(20.79)$$
$$= 561.3 \text{ kips}$$

Proportion flange force to splice plates:
Area of exterior plate = (5/8)(16)   = 10 in^2
Area of interior plate = (5/8)(6.5)(2) = 8.13 in^2

Since the splice plate areas differ by <u>more than 10%</u>, the force
must be proportioned by ratio of plate area.

Exterior plate force = (561.3)(10)/(10 + 8.13)   Art. 6.13.6.1.4c,
                        = 309.6 kips   Commentary p. 6-240

Interior plate force = (561.3)(8.13)/(10 + 8.13)
                        = 251.7 kips

703. **(Continued)**

Check splice plate size:

Outside plate:

$$W_n = 16.0 - (4)(1) + (2)(3.5)^2 / [(4)(3.5)]$$
$$= 13.75 \text{ in.}$$

$$A_n = 13.75 \times 5/8" = 8.59 \text{ in}^2 > 0.85 \, A_g \quad \text{Governs.}$$

$$0.85 \, A_g = 0.85(10) = 8.5 \text{ in}^2 \hspace{4cm} \text{Art. 6.13.5.2}$$

$$\therefore A_n = 8.5 \text{ in}^2$$

Inside plate:

$$W_n = 2\left\{ 6.5 - (2)(1) + (3.5)^2 / [(4)(3.5)] \right\}$$
$$= 10.75 \text{ in.}$$

$$A_n = 10.75 \times 5/8" = 6.72 \text{ in}^2 < 0.85 \, A_g$$

$$0.85 \, A_g = 0.85(8.13) = 6.91 \hspace{3cm} \text{OK}$$

$$\therefore A_n = 6.72 \text{ in}^2$$

For tension:
For yielding: Eq. 6.8.2.1-1

Outside $P_r = \phi_y F_y A_g = (0.95)(36 \text{ ksi})(10 \text{ in}^2) = 342 \text{ kips} > 309.6 \text{ kips}$ OK

Inside $P_r = \phi_y F_y A_g = (0.95)(36 \text{ ksi})(8.13 \text{ in}^2) = 278.0 \text{ kips} > 251.7 \text{ kips}$ OK

For fracture: Eq. 6.8.2.1-2

Outside $P_r = \phi_u F_u A_n U = (0.8)(58 \text{ ksi})(8.5 \text{ in}^2)(1.0) = 394.4 \text{ kips} > 309.6 \text{ kips}$ OK

Inside $P_r = \phi_u F_u A_n U = (0.8)(58 \text{ ksi})(6.72 \text{ in}^2)(1.0) = 311.8 \text{ kips} > 251.7 \text{ kips}$ OK

For compression:
$R_r = \phi_c F_y A_s$ where $A_s = A_g$ Eq. 6.13.6.1.4c-4

Outside $R_r = (0.9)(36 \text{ ksi})(10) = 324 \text{ kips} > 309.6 \text{ kips}$ OK

Inside $R_r = (0.9)(36 \text{ ksi})(8.13) = 263.4 \text{ kips} > 251.7 \text{ kips}$ OK

703. **(Continued)**

(b) Verify the number of bolts in the flange splice, and revise the number if required.

Check flange bolts:

Maximum distance between end fasteners = 3.5 in. × 7 spaces = 24.5 in. < 50 in. so 20% decrease in bolt strength per Art. 6.13.2.7 is not required.

By specification, the bolt threads are included in the shear plane; hence the bolt strength from Eq. 6.13.2.7-2 will be used directly.

Bolt shear strength:

$R_n = 0.38 A_b F_{ub} N_s$ Eq. 6.13.2.7-2

$F_{ub} = 120$ ksi   Art. 6.4.3.1

$R_n = 0.38(0.6)(120)(1) = 27.4$ kips   Bolt strength controls over bearing strength

Bolt bearing strength:

F_u = 58 ksi M-270, Gr 36 steel

L_c = 2 – (1-in.-dia./2)   Clear distance from edge of hole to edge of connected plate

     = 1.5 in. < 2d = 1.75 in.

d = 7/8 in.   Nominal bolt diameter

t = 5/8 in. or 1.26 in.   Thickness of connected material

$R_n = 1.2 L_c t F_u$ Eq. 6.13.2.9-2

Bearing on splice plates:

ϕR_n = (0.8)(1.2)(1.5)(5/8)(58) where ϕ_{bb} = 0.8

     = 52.2 kips per bolt   Does not control bolt strength

Bearing on beam flange:

ϕR_n = (0.8)(1.2)(1.5)(1.26)(58)

     = 105.2 kips per bolt   Does not control bolt strength

Required number of bolts:

At outside plate = (27.4 kips per bolt)(16 bolts)   Single shear per plate

               = 438.4 kips > 309.6 kips   OK

At inside plates = (27.4 kips per bolt)(16 bolts)   Single shear per plate

               = 438.4 kips > 251.7 kips   OK

703. (Continued)

Check resistance:

Art 6.13.2.7
6.13.2.2 through 6.13.5

$F_s = f_s/R_h$ Eq. 6.13.6.1.4c-5

f_s = maximum flexural stress due to Service II load combination at the mid-thickness of the flange under consideration for the smaller section at the point of splice.

$M_{SII} = DC + DW + 1.3 (LL + IM)$
$\quad\quad = -69 + 26 + 1.3(730) = 906 \text{ ft-kips}$

$f_s \quad = (906)(12)/(885)$
$\quad\quad = 12.28 \text{ ksi}$

$R_h \quad = 1.0$ Homogeneous girder
$P_{fs} \quad = F_s A_g$
$A_g \quad = 20.79 \text{ in}^2$ Previously calculated

$P_{fs} \quad = (12.28 \text{ ksi}/1.0) (20.79)$
$\quad\quad = 255.3 \text{ kips}$

Bolt slip resistance:

$R_n \quad = K_h K_s N_s P_t$ Eq. 6.13.2.8-1
$\quad\quad = (1.0)(0.33)(2)(39) = 25.7 \text{ kips}$

For 16 bolts,

$R_n \quad = 16(25.74) = 411.84 \text{ kips}$
$R_r \quad = \phi R_n = (1.0)(411.84) = 411.8 \text{ kips} > 255.3 \text{ kips} \quad\quad \text{OK}$

Thus the splice bolts are satisfactory as designed for strength. Since the force in the compression flange is the same, no additional check of the bolts on that flange is necessary, and the connection is symmetrical.

LATERAL FORCES

LATERAL FORCES EXAM SPECIFICATIONS

- The 4-hour **Lateral Forces (Wind/Earthquake)** breadth examination is offered on Saturday morning and focuses on wind/earthquake loads. It contains 40 multiple-choice questions.

- The exam uses the US Customary System (USCS) of units.

- The exam is developed with questions that will require a variety of approaches and methodologies, including design, analysis, and application.

- The knowledge areas specified as examples of kinds of knowledge are not exclusive or exhaustive categories.

- Score results are combined with depth exam results for final score of this component.

	Approximate Number of Questions

I. Analysis of Structures — **15**

  A. Lateral Forces — 4
    1. Wind
    2. Horizontal seismic
    3. Vertical seismic
    4. Dynamic earth pressure

  B. Lateral Force Distribution — 9
    1. Statics (e.g., determinate and indeterminate, location of forces and moments, free-body diagrams)
    2. Seismic design categories (C and lower)
    3. Seismic design categories (D and higher)
    4. Seismic static force procedures
    5. Seismic dynamic force procedures
    6. Configuration of a structural system to resist effects of horizontal torsional moments
    7. Relative rigidity force distribution
    8. Horizontal/plan and vertical irregularities
    9. Flexible diaphragms
    10. Rigid diaphragms
    11. Simplified wind
    12. Wind analytic procedures
    13. Wind components and cladding
    14. Main wind force resisting systems

  C. Methods — 2
    1. Computer-generated structural analysis techniques (e.g., modeling, interpreting, and verifying results)
    2. Simplified analysis methods (e.g., influence lines, portal frame method/cantilever method)

II. Design and Detailing of Structures   **24**
  A. General Structural Considerations   3
    1. Load combinations
    2. Serviceability requirements: building drift
    3. Anchorage of a structural system to resist uplift and sliding forces
    4. Components, attachments, and cladding
    5. Redundancy factors
    6. Overstrength
    7. Ductility requirements
    8. Abutment/pier seat width
  B. Structural Systems Integration   2
    1. Structural systems to resist effects of lateral forces
    2. Constructability
    3. Strengthening existing systems: seismic retrofit
      a. Details
      b. System compatibility
  C. Structural Steel   4
    1. Ordinary moment frames
    2. Intermediate moment-resisting frames
    3. Special moment-resisting frames
    4. Bracing
    5. Ordinary concentric braced frames
    6. Special concentric braced frames
    7. Eccentric braced frames
    8. Bridge piers
  D. Light Gage/Cold-Formed Steel   1
    1. Metal deck diaphragms
    2. Light-framed wall systems (e.g., shearwall systems)
  E. Concrete   5
    1. Ordinary or intermediate shear walls
    2. Special shear walls
    3. Ordinary or intermediate moment-resisting frames
    4. Special moment-resisting frames
    5. Diaphragms
    6. Reinforcement details (e.g., ductile detailing, anchorage)
    7. Bridge piers
    8. Tilt-up construction
  F. Wood   3
    1. Shear walls
    2. Plywood diaphragms (e.g., drag struts, chords)
    3. Plywood sub-diaphragms
  G. Masonry   3
    1. Flexural-compression members
    2. Slender walls
    3. Ordinary or intermediate shear walls
    4. Special shear walls
    5. Anchorage for walls (e.g., out-of-plane)
    6. Attachment of elements to masonry

H. Foundations and Retaining Structures   3
   1. Spread footings
   2. Piles (concrete, steel, timber)
   3. Drilled shafts/drilled piers/caissons

III. Construction Administration   1
A. Structural observation

Lateral Forces (Wind/Earthquake) Component of the Structural DEPTH Exam Specifications

Effective Beginning with the April 2011 Examination

The 4-hour **Lateral Forces (Wind/Earthquake)** depth examination is offered on Saturday afternoon. The depth modules of the Structural Engineering exam focus on a single area of practice in structural engineering. Examinees must choose either the **BUILDINGS** or the **BRIDGES** module. Examinees must work the same module on both components. That is, if bridges is the module chosen in the Vertical Forces component, then bridges must be the module chosen in the Lateral Forces component. All questions are constructed response (essay).

The exam uses the US Customary System (USCS) of units.

BUILDINGS

The **Lateral Forces (Wind/Earthquake)** Structural Engineering depth exam in **BUILDINGS** covers lateral forces, lateral force distribution, analysis methods, general structural considerations (element design), structural systems integration (connections), and foundations and retaining structures. This 4-hour module contains one problem from each of the following areas:

- Steel structure
- Concrete structure
- Wood and/or masonry structure
- General analysis (e.g., existing structures, secondary structures, nonbuilding structures, and/or computer verification)

All problems are equally weighted.

At least two problems include seismic content at Seismic Design Category D and above.
At least one problem includes wind content of at least 110 mph.
Problems may include a multistory building.
Problems may include a foundation.

BRIDGES

The **Lateral Forces (Wind/Earthquake)** Structural Engineering depth exam in **BRIDGES** covers gravity loads, superstructures, substructures, and lateral forces and may test pedestrian bridge and/or vehicular bridge knowledge. This 4-hour module contains three problems, one from each of the following areas:

- Columns (25% of your score)
- Footings (25% of your score)
- General analysis (i.e., seismic and/or wind) (50% of your score)

LATERAL FORCES AM PRACTICE EXAM

101. The following information is for a building that is located in a seismic zone.

Design Code:
ASCE 7: *Minimum Design Loads for Buildings and Other Structures,* 2010.

Design Data:

Site shear wave velocity for the top 100 ft, $\bar{v}_s$	1,100 ft/sec
Mapped spectral response acceleration at 0.2-sec period, S_S	1.00
Mapped spectral response acceleration at 1-sec period, S_1	0.45
Building period, T	0.80 sec
Long-period transition period, T_L	8 sec

Assumption:
No clay, peat, or liquefiable soils

The design spectral response acceleration S_a is most nearly:

- (A) 1.10
- (B) 0.73
- (C) 0.58
- (D) 0.47

Copyright 2014 by NCEES   134   GO ON TO THE NEXT PAGE

102. The figure shows a diagram for an agricultural building.

Design Codes:
   IBC: *International Building Code,* 2012 edition (without supplements).
   ASCE 7: *Minimum Design Loads for Buildings and Other Structures,* 2010.

Design Data:
   Basic wind speed, V
      Risk Category I   120 mph
      Risk Category II   132 mph
      Risk Category III-IV   143 mph

Assumptions:
   Topographic factor, K_{zt} = 1.0
   Building is located in flat open country.

The wind velocity pressure (psf) at mean roof height for MWFRS is most nearly:

(A)   21.9
(B)   27.4
(C)   33.2
(D)   40.0

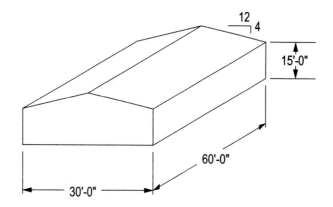

103. The figure shows a roof plan view of a single-story precast concrete building.

Design Data:
  The wind load W is 640 plf.
  In-plane design shear strength of the connection $\phi V_N = 8.5$ kips.
  All four exterior walls are shear walls.
  The wind load is applied at the diaphragm elevation.
  Type B connectors are uniformly spaced on the east and west walls.

The number of Type B connectors between a single 8-ft × 60-ft roof panel and the wall is most nearly:

(A)   two

(B)   three

(C)   four

(D)   six

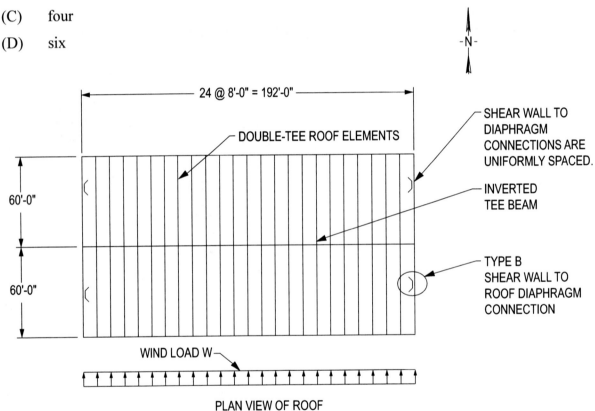

PLAN VIEW OF ROOF

104. The figure shows a line diagram for a three-story steel-framed hospital building.

Design Codes:
IBC: *International Building Code,* 2012 edition (without supplements).
ASCE 7: *Minimum Design Loads for Buildings and Other Structures,* 2010.

Design Data:
S_1 0.15
S_s 1.0
Site class   C
T_L 8 sec

Assumption:
The building lateral force resisting system is concentrically braced frames.

The seismic base shear (kips) is most nearly:

(A)   138
(B)   208
(C)   267
(D)   383

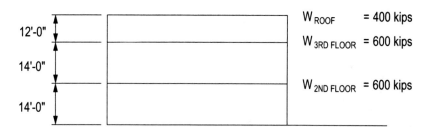

105. The figure shows the elevation view of a two-span continuous concrete bridge. The pier has two columns. The superstructure is restrained at the pier only.

Design Code:
   AASHTO LRFD Bridge Design Specifications, 6th edition, 2012.

Design Data:
   Average superstructure weight per foot (including parapet, future wearing surface, and portion of columns) = 10 kips/ft of superstructure over a length of 214 ft (210 ft center-to-center of abutment plus 2 ft each end).
   EI (single column) = 16×10^6 kips-ft^2

Assumptions:
   Columns are fixed at both ends.
   Acceleration of gravity = 32.2 ft/sec^2

Using the uniform load method, the period of vibration (sec) of the bridge in the longitudinal direction is most nearly:

(A)   0.25
(B)   0.36
(C)   0.50
(D)   0.66

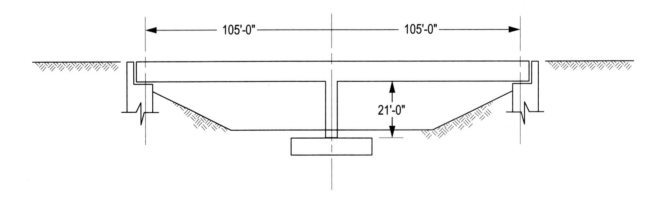

106. A two-span simply supported girder and slab bridge is shown in the figure.

Design Code:
   AASHTO LRFD Bridge Design Specifications, 6th edition, 2012.

Design Data:
   Wind direction is perpendicular to the structure.
   Wind velocity is 100 mph.

Assumptions:
   The pier and abutment bearings are restrained in the transverse direction.
   All bridge parts are less than 30 ft above low ground or water level.

The maximum unfactored moment (ft-kips) in the direction transverse to the bridge at the base of the pier due to wind load on the superstructure only is most nearly:

(A)   240
(B)   798
(C)   1,596
(D)   1,792

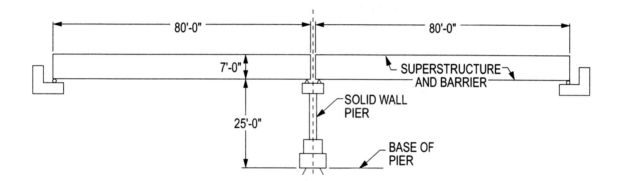

107. A sign and supporting pipe column are shown in the figure.

Design Data:
No earthquake forces
No ice buildup
Ignore pipe shape factor
Ignore torsion
Sign dead load   20 psf (ignore support arm)
Support pipe column:
    Weight   46.6 plf
    Area   13.7 in^2
    Section modulus   38.6 in^3
    Moment of inertia, $I_{x\text{-}x} = I_{y\text{-}y}$ 231 in^4
Wind forces $\perp$ to the sign:
    On sign face   60 psf
    On pipe column   60 plf

Assumption:
Wind load on sign face acts through geometric center of sign.

The maximum flexural and axial service load stress (ksi) in the pipe column when the complete sign/pipe column assembly is subjected to the dead and wind loads above is most nearly:

(A)   14.5
(B)   11.5
(C)   9.1
(D)   7.8

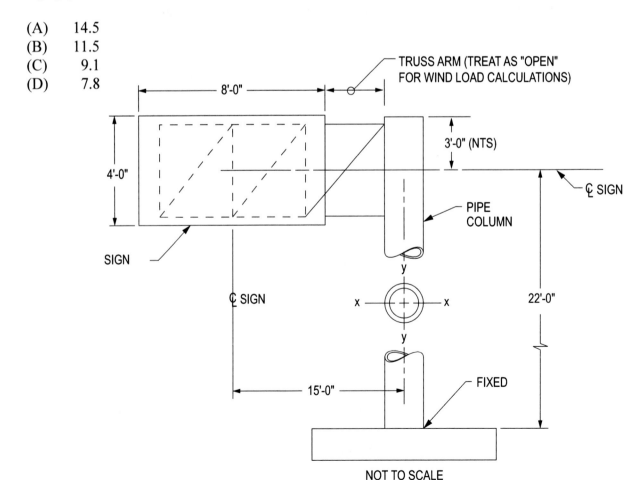

NOT TO SCALE

108. The figure shows the plan view of a tilt-up concrete wall warehouse roof.

Design Code:
   ASCE 7: *Minimum Design Loads for Buildings and Other Structures,* 2010.

Design Data:
Roof	26 ft, A.F.F.
Top of panel	26 ft, A.F.F.
Roof DL	15 psf
Panel DL	70 psf

Assumption:
   $C_s = 0.15$

The seismic chord force (kips) at Point A is most nearly:

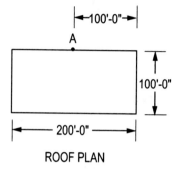

ROOF PLAN

(A)   11.3
(B)   21.1
(C)   24.9
(D)   45.5

109. The figure shows the plan for a rigid floor diaphragm.

Design Codes:
   IBC: *International Building Code,* 2012 edition (without supplements).
   ASCE 7: *Minimum Design Loads for Buildings and Other Structures,* 2010.

Design Data:
   There are shear walls on all four sides.
   The calculated story seismic shear is 75 kips.
   The calculated center of gravity is shown.

The total torsion (ft-kips) to be distributed to the shear walls is most nearly:

(A)   0
(B)   375
(C)   563
(D)   750

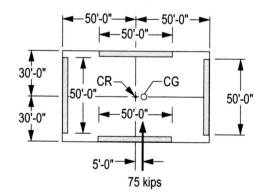

110. The building shown in the figure is subjected to seismic force in N-S direction.

Design Code:
ASCE 7: *Minimum Design Loads for Buildings and Other Structures,* 2010.

Design Data:
Roof DL	15 psf
Wall weight	75 psf
Seismic coefficient, C_s	0.20 in the N-S direction

Assumptions:
Flexible roof diaphragm.
Neglect openings in walls.

The drag force (lb) in the drag member A is most nearly:

(A) 10,800
(B) 16,800
(C) 19,500
(D) 21,300

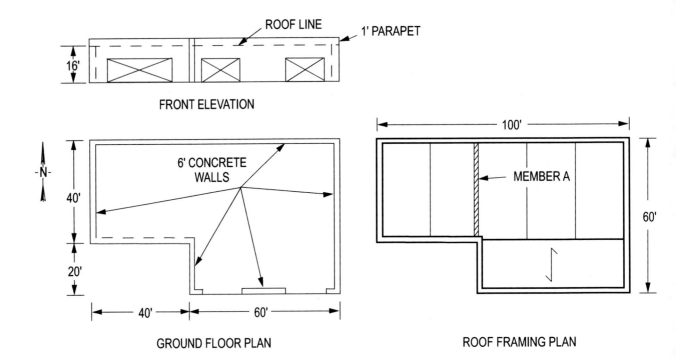

FRONT ELEVATION

GROUND FLOOR PLAN

ROOF FRAMING PLAN

111. The building shown in the figure is in Seismic Design Category D.

Design Code:
  ASCE 7: *Minimum Design Loads for Buildings and Other Structures,* 2010.

Assumption:
  Rigid roof diaphragm.

Which horizontal structural irregularity does it have?

(A)   Torsional irregularity only

(B)   Reentrant corner irregularity only

(C)   Both torsional irregularity and reentrant corner irregularity

(D)   No irregularities.

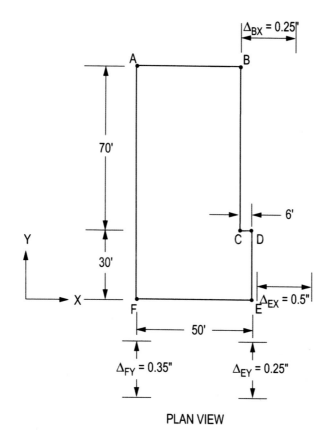

PLAN VIEW

112. The figure shows a building with four braced frames and the corresponding seismic forces, E, in the two perpendicular directions.

Design Code:
    ASCE 7: *Minimum Design Loads for Buildings and Other Structures,* 2010.

Design Data:
    Seismic Design Category D

Assumptions:
    Neglect the vertical seismic load effects given in ASCE 7 12.4.2.2.
    Redundancy factor ρ is 1.0.
    Load combinations of ASCE 7 12.4.3 are not required.

The maximum axial force (kips) in Column AD due to seismic forces E is most nearly:

(A)   16.0
(B)   16.8
(C)   19.6
(D)   28.0

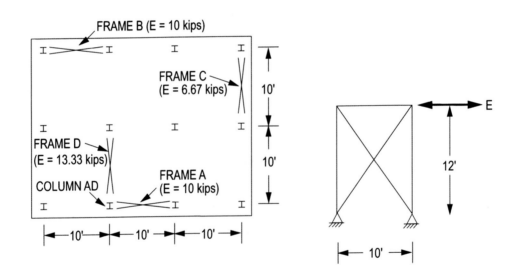

113. The figures show the roof plan and cross section for a one-story building.

Assumption:
   The roof diaphragm is flexible.

The chord force (kips) in the north wall due to the wind forces in the north-south direction is most nearly:

(A)   0.19
(B)   1.47
(C)   4.12
(D)   8.23

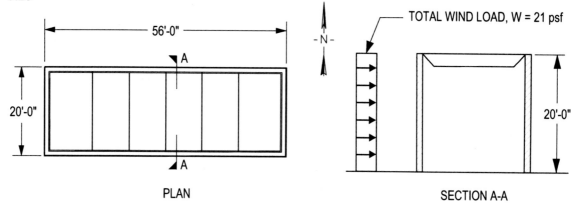

PLAN

SECTION A-A

114. The figure shows a section at a pier of a multispan, continuous slab bridge.

Design Code:
   AASHTO LRFD Bridge Design Specifications, 6th edition, 2012.

Assumptions:
   Seismic Zone 4
   Columns are fixed at top and bottom.
   Response modification factor, R = 1.0

The maximum moment (ft-kips) in each column due to the 50-kip transverse horizontal load at the pier is most nearly:

(A)   25
(B)   250
(C)   500
(D)   1,000

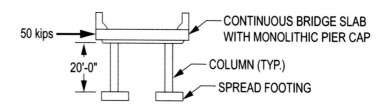

115. The computer-generated maximum and minimum vertical support reactions are given for Node 1 of Frame A. These vertical reactions were calculated based on all applicable load combinations in ASCE 7, Chapter 2.

Design Data:
    Dead load   200 plf
    Live load   200 plf

Node 1	Maximum (kips)	Minimum (kips)
ASD	9.5	−6.3
LRFD	16.9	−10.7

The service level wind force F_W (kips) at the top of Frame A is most nearly:

(A)   6
(B)   10
(C)   11
(D)   20

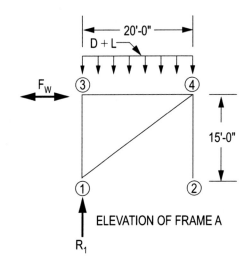

ELEVATION OF FRAME A

116. The ductility of a reinforced-concrete frame building is reduced by:

(A)   providing larger-sized reinforcing bars than those required by design analysis

(B)   providing continuous reinforcement at column joints

(C)   substituting column spirals for column ties

(D)   providing sufficient development lengths for the reinforcing bars

117. An ordinary concentric braced frame that is part of a detention facility is shown in the figure.

Design Codes:
    IBC: *International Building Code,* 2012 edition (without supplements).
    ASCE 7: *Minimum Design Loads for Buildings and Other Structures,* 2010.

Assumption:
    The attached building components are not designed to accommodate story drift.

The allowable seismic drift (in.) for the first level is most nearly:

(A)   0.3
(B)   1.4
(C)   3.6
(D)   4.8

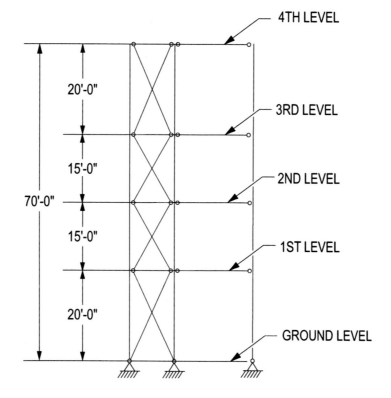

118. Lateral wind loads on a bridge are given below.

Design Code:
   AASHTO LRFD Bridge Design Specifications, 6th edition, 2012.

Design Data:
   Unfactored wind loads:
   On structure = 60 kips
   On vehicles = 10 kips

Assumption:
   $\eta = 1.0$

The maximum strength limit state factored load for wind forces (kips) is most nearly:

(A)   30
(B)   70
(C)   80
(D)   100

119. The figure shows a three-span continuous highway bridge that is constructed in a seismic region.

Design Code:
   AASHTO LRFD Bridge Design Specifications, 6th edition, 2012.

Assumptions:
   The horizontal deflection of the bridge deck in the longitudinal direction is 0.0107 ft due to a 1-kip/ft force acting along the deck.
   The weight per foot of the bridge including half of the substructure is 8.8 kips/ft.
   The acceleration of gravity is 32.2 ft/sec².

Using the single-mode spectral analysis method, the period of the bridge (sec) in the longitudinal direction is most nearly:

(A)   0.17
(B)   0.26
(C)   0.34
(D)   0.50

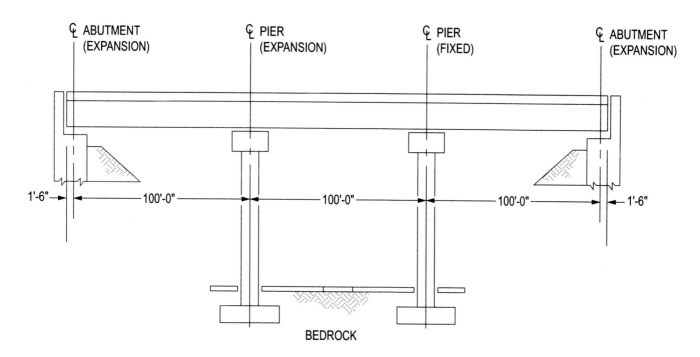

GO ON TO THE NEXT PAGE

120. The following data apply to a 1,500-ft^2 office building in a seismic zone.

Design Code:
ASCE 7: *Minimum Design Loads for Buildings and Other Structures,* 2010.

Design Data:
Seismic Design Category D
Building height = 175 ft

Assumptions:
No irregularities.
Maximum lateral force in any one plane of lateral resisting elements is 50% of the total lateral force.

Which of the following systems is **not** allowed?

(A)   Special reinforced concrete shear walls

(B)   Special steel concentrically braced frames

(C)   Special steel moment frames

(D)   Special reinforced masonry shear walls

121. The figure shows a braced frame connection at the beam/brace location.

Design Code:
AISC: *Seismic Design Manual,* 2nd edition.

Design Data:
ASTM A53 pipe steel braces.

Assumption:
Special concentrically braced frame designed per AISC *Seismic Design Manual.*

The vertical portion of the earthquake effect E (kips) in the beam at the point of the connection is most nearly:

(A)   117
(B)   133
(C)   146
(D)   186

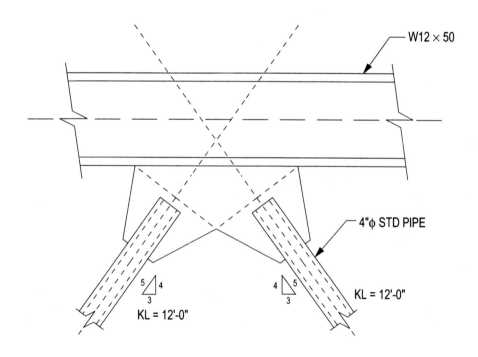

GO ON TO THE NEXT PAGE

122. A 2,000-ft^2 retail facility is located in a seismic zone.

Design Code:
   AISC: *Seismic Design Manual,* 2nd edition.

Which of the following is **not** required for an intermediate moment frame?

(A)   The connection shall be capable of resisting a minimum interstory drift angle of 0.04 radian.

(B)   The region of the beam subject to inelastic straining shall be treated as a protected zone.

(C)   Both flanges of the beams shall be braced at a distance not to exceed 0.17 r_y E/F_y.

(D)   I-shaped beams and columns shall have b/t $\leq 0.38\sqrt{E/F_y}$

123. The figure shows a steel ordinary moment frame.

Design Code:
   AISC: *Steel Construction Manual,* 14th edition.

Assumptions:
   The connection between the beam and column is a moment connection.
   The columns are laterally braced in the plane perpendicular to the frame at the beam-column joint.

The effective length required for stability check for Column 1 and Column 2 is most nearly:

(A)   0.65 L
(B)   1.00 L
(C)   1.20 L
(D)   2.00 L

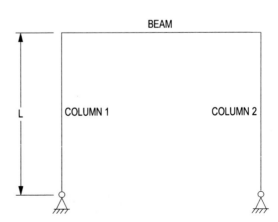

124. An office building is supported by special concentrically braced frames.

Design Code:
   AISC: *Seismic Design Manual,* 2nd edition.

Design Data:
   Seismic Design Category D
   A500 Grade B hollow structural section tubes.

Assumption:
   Amplified seismic brace force = 175 kips.

The required tensile strength of the bracing connection (kips) is most nearly:

	ASD	LRFD
(A)	60	90
(B)	80	120
(C)	105	160
(D)	120	175

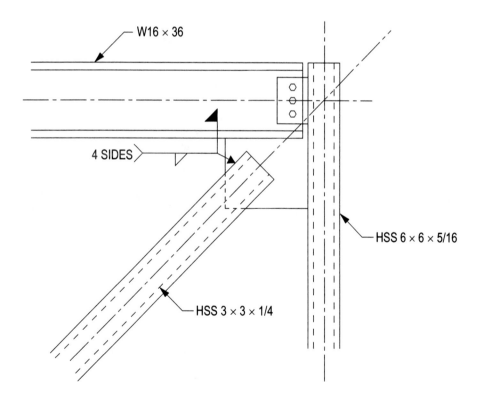

125. The end condition of a braced wall is shown in the figure.

Design Codes:
   AISI: *North American Specification for the Design of Cold-Formed Steel Structural Members*, 2007 edition with Supplement No. 2 (2010).
   ASCE 7: *Minimum Design Loads for Buildings and Other Structures*, 2010.

Design Data:
   Tension force, T = 2 kips (strength level seismic load)
   F_u = 62 ksi for connection plate and strap brace material
   Material thickness of connection plate and strap brace = 0.0566 in.

Assumptions:
   Connection plate is adequately attached to wall framing, and wall is adequately attached to foundation.
   Minimum spacing and edge distance requirements for the screws in the connection are satisfied.
   Use ASD or LRFD.

The minimum number of 1/8-in.-diameter screws required to connect the strap brace to the connection plate is:

   (A)   2
   (B)   4
   (C)   6
   (D)   8

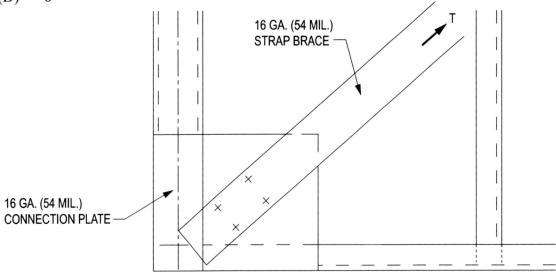

126. The figures show an elevation view and a plan view of a bridge pier founded in rock.

Design Code:
   AASHTO LRFD Bridge Design Specifications, 6th edition, 2012.

Design Data:
   Factored transverse force applied at top of pier cap   39 kips
   Factored longitudinal force applied at top of pier cap   16 kips
   Factored total vertical load from superstructure applied to pier   740 kips
   Factored dead load of pier   195 kips

Assumption:
   Neglect earth load.

The maximum factored contact pressure (ksf) for the structural design of the foundation on rock is most nearly:

(A)   6.0
(B)   5.2
(C)   4.8
(D)   3.9

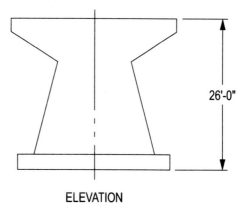

ELEVATION

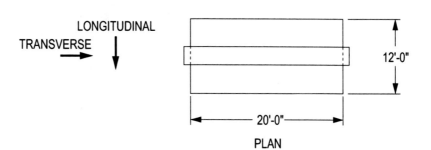

PLAN

127. The figure shows a detail of a structure with a plywood diaphragm roof and tilt-up concrete bearing/shear walls.

Design Codes:
   IBC: *International Building Code*, 2012 edition (without supplements).
   ASCE 7: *Minimum Design Loads for Buildings and Other Structures*, 2010.

Design Data:
   Concrete density = 130 pcf

Assumptions:
   $S_{DS} = 0.90$ g
   $I_e = 1.0$
   Seismic Design Category D
   $K_a = 2.0$

The anchorage force at each anchor F_p (kips) is most nearly:

(A)   2.1
(B)   1.7
(C)   1.3
(D)   1.0

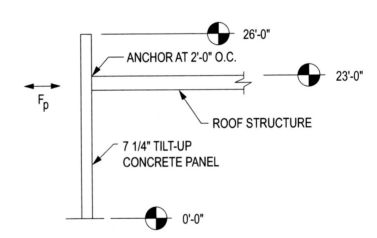

128. A concrete pier column is supported by a spread footing.

Design Code:
AASHTO LRFD Bridge Design Specifications, 6th edition, 2012.

Design Data:
f'_c = 4 ksi
f_y = 60 ksi

Assumptions:
Bridge is in Seismic Zone 3.
All applicable modification factors should be included for development length.
Normal weight concrete.
Uncoated reinforcing steel.

The development length (in.) into the footing for the vertical column reinforcing is most nearly:

(A)   30
(B)   36
(C)   45
(D)   60

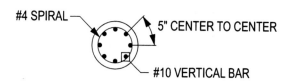

SECTION A-A

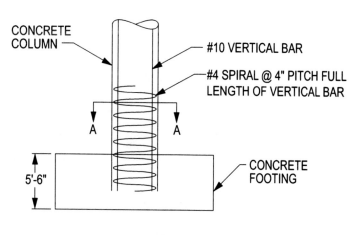

FOOTING ELEVATION

129. A cast-in-place concrete wall is to be constructed at a location where there is a low exterior grade. The wall is to be pinned at the interior slab-on-grade for wind design.

Assumption:
    Pre-made formwork cannot be modified.

Which of the following details shown could be used to construct the wall in a practical manner?

(A)   1 and 2

(B)   2 and 3

(C)   1 and 3

(D)   2 and 4

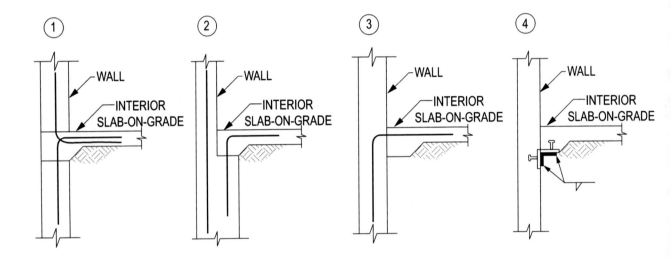

130. The figure shows a 16-in. × 16-in. concrete column of a multistory unbraced reinforced concrete frame.

Design Code:
    ACI 318: *Building Code Requirements for Structural Concrete*, 2011.

For the given factored moments in the column, the maximum factored shear (kips) in the column is most nearly:

(A)   2.8
(B)   3.8
(C)   4.3
(D)   10.4

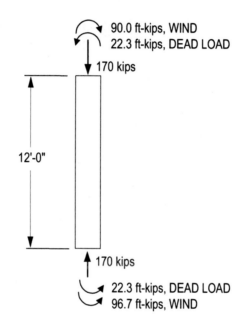

131. The roof diaphragm of a single-story building is shown in the figure.

Design Code:
  NDS: *National Design Specification for Wood Construction ASD/LRFD*, 2012 edition & *National Design Specification Supplement, Design Values for Wood Construction*, 2012 edition.

Design Data:
  $\lambda = 1.0$ if LRFD method is used.
  Wind load, W = 333 plf

Assumption:
  $C_M = C_t = C_g = C_\Delta = C_{eg} = C_{di} = C_{tn} = 1.0$

The number of 10d common nails required on each side of the splice to connect the two 2× Spruce Pine-Fir top plates together for the diaphragm chord force at Point A is most nearly:

	ASD	**LRFD**
(A)	25	31
(B)	30	37
(C)	39	48
(D)	47	58

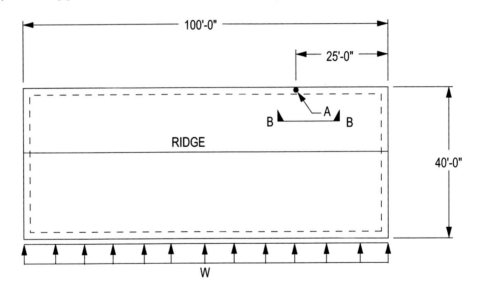

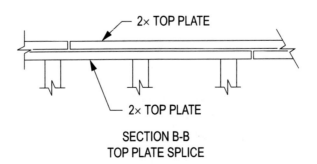

SECTION B-B
TOP PLATE SPLICE

132. A plywood shear wall with horizontal seismic loads is shown in the figure.

Design Data:
    All dead loads have been reduced.
    All seismic loads are at service level.

Assumption:
    All vertical seismic loads are being resisted by the outer shear wall chords.

The uplift force (kips) on the holddown is most nearly:

(A)   0
(B)   2.25
(C)   5.75
(D)   8.10

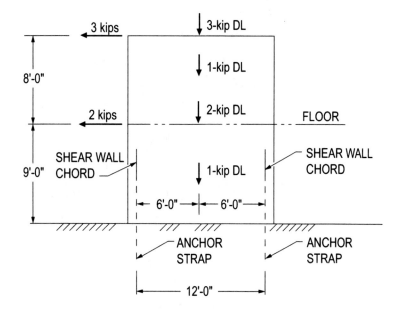

ELEVATION OF PLYWOOD SHEAR WALL

133. The figure shows a roof plan of a building.

Design Codes:
    IBC: *International Building Code*, 2012 edition (without supplements).
    ASCE 7: *Minimum Design Loads for Buildings and Other Structures*, 2010.

Design Data:
    Seismic Design Category D

Assumption:
    The glulam headers above the glazing are active chord members of the roof diaphragm.

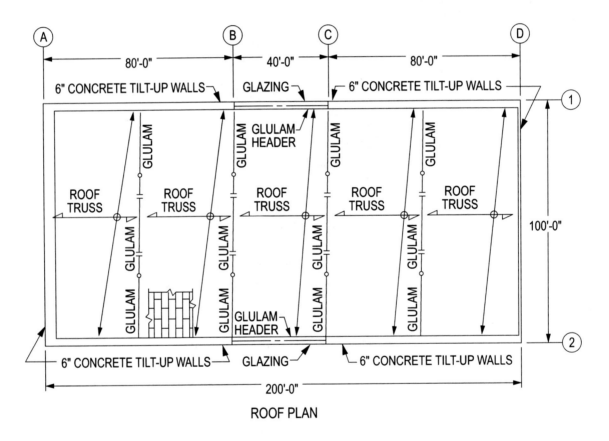

ROOF PLAN

133. (Continued)

The best connection of the glulam header to the wall panel (shown in elevation view) is most nearly:

(A)

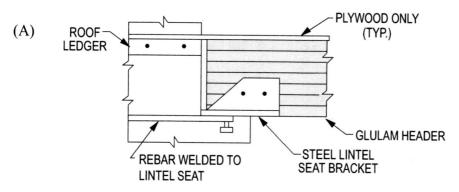

(B)

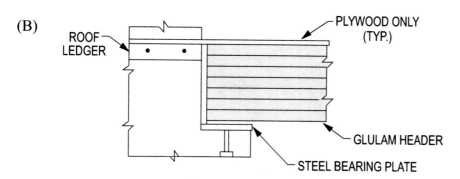

(C)

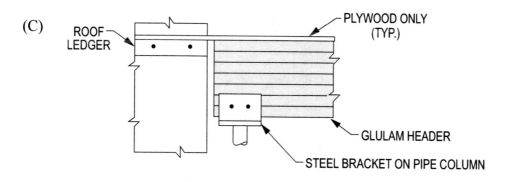

(D)

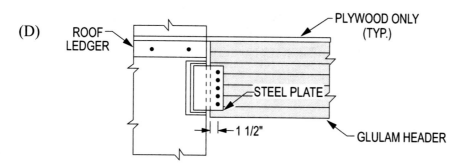

134. The unreinforced masonry interior partition wall shown in the figure is subjected to seismic loads and its own dead weight.

Design Codes:
  TMS 402/602: *Building Code Requirements and Specifications for Masonry Structures* (and related commentaries), 2011.
  ASCE 7: *Minimum Design Loads for Buildings and Other Structures*, 2010.

Design Data:
  Wall dead load   55 psf (of wall area)
  Horizontal seismic force, F_p 17 psf
  $S_{DS} = 1.0$ g
  Hollow concrete masonry units
  Type S mortar, face shell bedded only
  Ungrouted, unreinforced
  Face shell width = 1 1/2"

Assumptions:
  Use allowable stress design.
  Mortar joint is "flush" joint. (Faces of mortar are flush with face shell of CMU.)

Using ASD, the net tensile stress (psi) on the masonry at mid-height of the wall is most nearly:

(A)   37.7
(B)   33.2
(C)   7.0
(D)   0.7

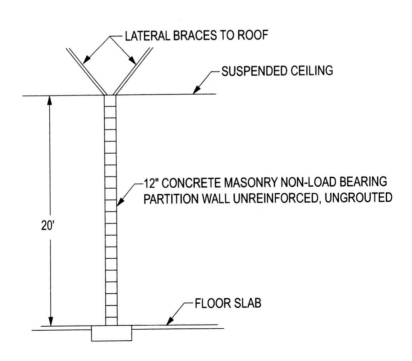

LATERAL BRACES TO ROOF

SUSPENDED CEILING

12" CONCRETE MASONRY NON-LOAD BEARING PARTITION WALL UNREINFORCED, UNGROUTED

20'

FLOOR SLAB

164

135. The figure shows an 8-in. reinforced concrete masonry wall.

Design Data:

Roof dead load	15 psf
Roof snow load	40 psf (non-reducible)
Average wall dead load	54 psf
Wind load (pressure or suction)	33 psf

Assumptions:
Roof dead load and snow loads act at joist-to-ledger connection.
Seismic forces do not govern.

For the load combination D + 0.75(0.6W) + 0.75S, the maximum design moment (ft-lb/ft) for the masonry wall is most nearly:

(A) 105
(B) 360
(C) 435
(D) 600

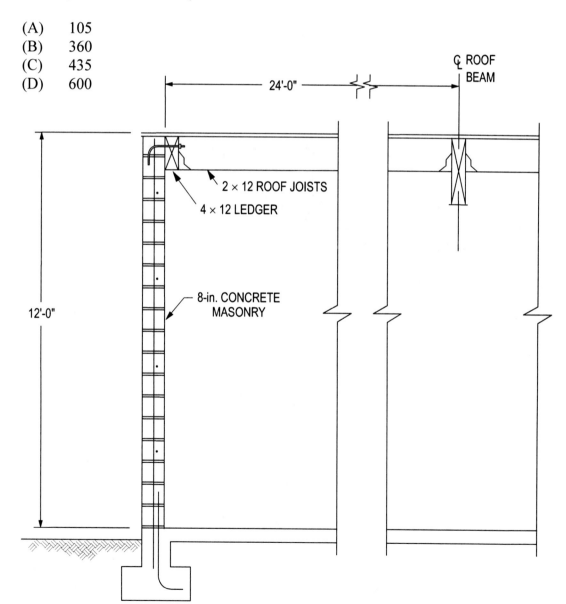

165

GO ON TO THE NEXT PAGE

136. A 3,000-ft^2 retail structure has a clear-spanning wood roof bearing on reinforced masonry bearing/shear walls.

Design Code:
ASCE 7: *Minimum Design Loads for Buildings and Other Structures*, 2010.

Assumptions:
$S_{DS} = 0.6\,g$
$S_{D1} = 0.2\,g$

The seismic base shear for equivalent lateral force procedure design (W is the weight of the structure) is most nearly:

(A) 0.300 W
(B) 0.120 W
(C) 0.080 W
(D) 0.040 W

137. An 8-in. CMU flanged shear wall and footing are shown in the figure.

Design Data:
Concentric dead load   560 kips (including footing weight)
Seismic overturning moment   2,304 ft-kips
All loads are at service level.

The maximum soil bearing pressure (ksf) is most nearly:

(A) 3.5
(B) 5.0
(C) 5.4
(D) 6.2

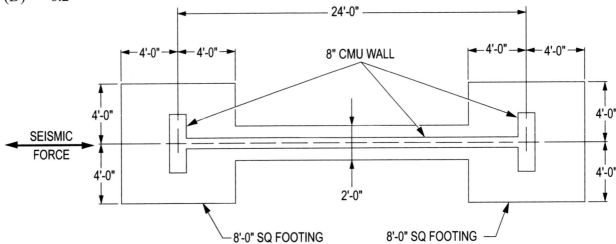

138. The figure shows column pile caps interconnected by a grade beam that acts as a seismic tie.

Design Code:
   IBC: *International Building Code,* 2012 edition (without supplements).

Design Data:
   Seismic Design Category D
   $S_{DS} = 0.75$ g

Assumption:
   Ignore weight of pile cap

The design strength force P (kips) to be resisted by the grade beam in tension or compression is most nearly:

(A)   0
(B)   21
(C)   25
(D)   60

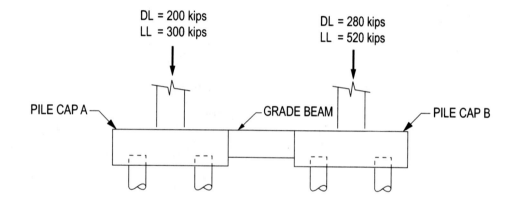

139. The figure shows a section through a concrete highway bridge that has two equal spans.

Design Code:
   AASHTO LRFD Bridge Design Specifications, 6th edition, 2012.

Design Data:
   Each span length   70 ft
   Base wind velocity   100 mph

Assumptions:
   The superstructure is rigidly connected to the pier cap.
   The bridge is not skewed.
   Neglect wind on live load and substructure.
   Bridge has multiple spans.

The axial unfactored load (kips) applied at the top of an exterior pile due to transverse wind on the superstructure is most nearly:

(A)   14.7
(B)   7.4
(C)   5.9
(D)   2.5

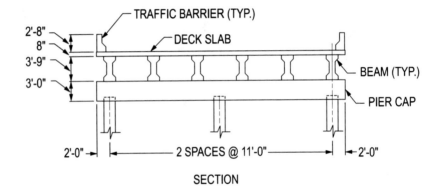

SECTION

140. A structure is located in Seismic Design Category D. Which of the following would **not** require the enforcement of structural observations for seismic resistance?

(A)   Height of structure is 60 ft

(B)   Risk Category III

(C)   Observations designated by the design professional responsible for structural design

(D)   Observations required by a building official

This completes the morning session. Solutions begin on page 187.

LATERAL FORCES PM BUILDINGS PRACTICE EXAM

169

801. The preliminary design of a renovation of an existing single-story office building with a wood roof framing system and masonry exterior walls is shown in **Figure 801.**

Design Codes:
IBC: *International Building Code,* 2012 edition (without supplements).
ASCE 7: *Minimum Design Loads for Buildings and Other Structures,* 2010.
TMS 402/602: *Building Code Requirements and Specifications for Masonry Structures* (and Related Commentaries), 2011.

Design Data:
Wind load	142 mph, Exposure C $K_{zt} = 1.67$
Seismic load	$S_{DS} = 0.70$
Masonry	$f'_m = 1,500$ psi Weight = 60 psf $f_y = 60,000$ psi 8" partially grouted CMU

REQUIREMENTS:

On the actual exam, any sketches necessary for these requirements must be neatly drawn in your solution pamphlet.

(a) During the preliminary design phase, the existing building is to be checked for compliance with the 2012 IBC wind and seismic loads. List three items to be checked at each of the following: exterior CMU wall, roof framing, and foundation system (list 9 items total).

(b) Determine the design wind pressure and seismic design force on the parapet. For wind, neglect corner zones. Consider interior zones only.

(c) For a horizontal service level wind pressure of 100 psf, check whether #5 at 48" o.c. vertical reinforcement at the centerline of the wall is adequate for the parapet. Check both the shear stress and flexural stress of the reinforced CMU parapet.

(d) The roof diaphragm requires attachment to the masonry wall for an out-of-plane anchorage force of 420 plf. Neatly sketch a complete wall anchorage connection at 48" o.c. Identify all required components but do not design.

801. (Continued)

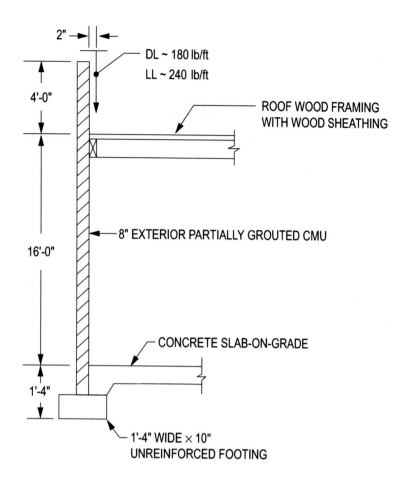

FIGURE 801

802. A two-story steel office building is shown in **Figure 802A.** The building has special concentrically braced frames on Column Lines A, E, 2, and 4 as shown in **Figure 802B.**

Design Codes:
  IBC: *International Building Code*, 2012 edition (without supplements).
  ASCE 7: *Minimum Design Loads for Buildings and Other Structures*, 2010.
  AISC: *Steel Construction Manual*, 14th edition.
  AISC: *Seismic Design Manual*, 2nd edition.

Design Data:
  Steel (columns and beams): ASTM A992, Grade 50.
  Steel braces: ASTM A53 Grade B
  Seismic Design Category D

Assumptions:
  Steel system is designed and detailed in accordance with AISC *Seismic Design Manual*.
  All braced frames have the same rigidity.
  $\rho = 1.0$
  Use workpoint-to-workpoint dimensions for member design.
  No torsional irregularities exist for the building.

REQUIREMENTS:

On the actual exam, any sketches necessary for these requirements must be neatly drawn in your solution pamphlet.

(a)   If the floor diaphragm shown in **Figure 802A** is a rigid diaphragm, determine the force in the braced frame on Grid 2 due to a 150-kip seismic story force acting in the E-W direction.

(b)   In **Figure 802B,** if the seismic forces $V_R = 40$ kips and $V_F = 40$ kips, design Brace 2 using a steel pipe section and ignoring the brace's own weight. The braces do not carry any gravity loads.

(c)   Without any calculations, neatly sketch an all-welded connection between Brace 2 and Column B-2 (W14), including connection to base plate and anchorage to foundation.

802. (Continued)

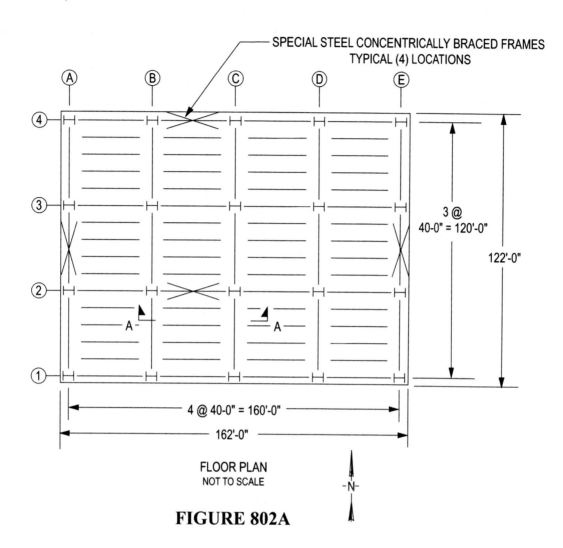

SPECIAL STEEL CONCENTRICALLY BRACED FRAMES
TYPICAL (4) LOCATIONS

3 @
40-0" = 120'-0"

122'-0"

4 @ 40-0" = 160'-0"

162'-0"

FLOOR PLAN
NOT TO SCALE

-N-

FIGURE 802A

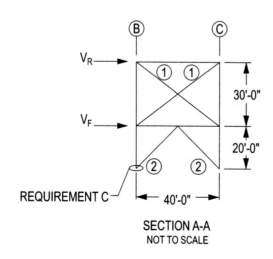

V_R

V_F

30'-0"

20'-0"

REQUIREMENT C

40'-0"

SECTION A-A
NOT TO SCALE

FIGURE 802B

803. A three-story concrete building is constructed with four special reinforced concrete shear walls as shown in **Figures 803A** and **803B.** Beams and columns on Lines B, C, 2, and 3 do not resist any lateral loads. All gravity loads are supported by the concrete frame system.

Design Codes:

        IBC: *International Building Code,* 2012 edition (without supplements).

        ASCE 7: *Minimum Design Loads for Buildings and Other Structures,* 2010.

        ACI 318: *Building Code Requirements for Structural Concrete,* 2011.

Design Data:

Level	Seismic Weight, W (kips)	Height, H (ft)
Roof	550	45
3rd	980	30
2nd	980	15
1st	—	0

$S_s = 0.52$

$S_1 = 0.18$

$I_e = 1.0$

Risk Category II

$\rho = 1.0$

Soil properties are unknown.

Concrete:

Foundations	$f'_c =$	3,000 psi
Columns and walls	$f'_c =$	5,000 psi
Reinforcing steel	$f_y =$	60,000 psi

Assumptions:

        The center of mass is at the center of the area.

        Assume period $T < T_L$

REQUIREMENTS:

On the actual exam, any sketches necessary for these requirements must be neatly drawn in your solution pamphlet.

(a) Determine the seismic base shear in the N-S direction. Use the equivalent lateral force procedure.

(b) Determine the seismic story force at each floor level.

(c) Determine if the footing dowels at the base of the concrete shear wall in **Figure 803C** are adequate for a factored in-plane seismic shear of 6.0 kips/ft. Check all governing criteria.

(d) Determine if the horizontal wall reinforcement in **Figure 803C** is adequate.

(e) If the contractor used dowels without hooks, briefly describe a possible repair solution.

803. (Continued)

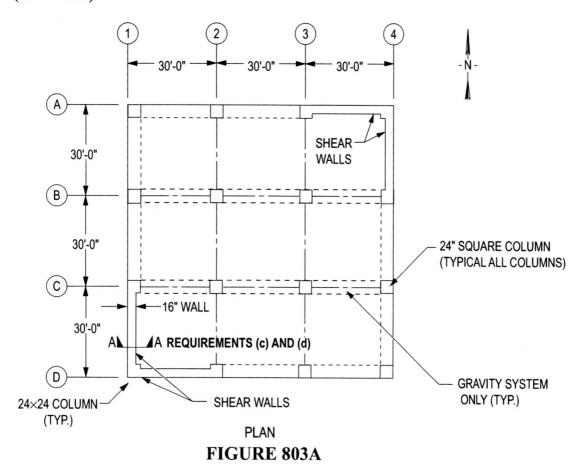

PLAN
FIGURE 803A

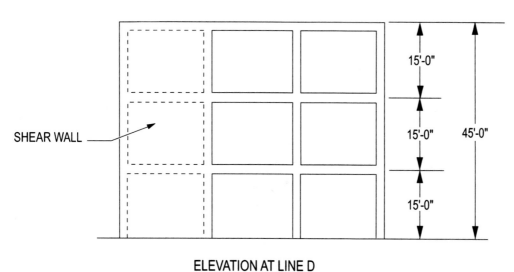

ELEVATION AT LINE D

FIGURE 803B

803. **(Continued)**

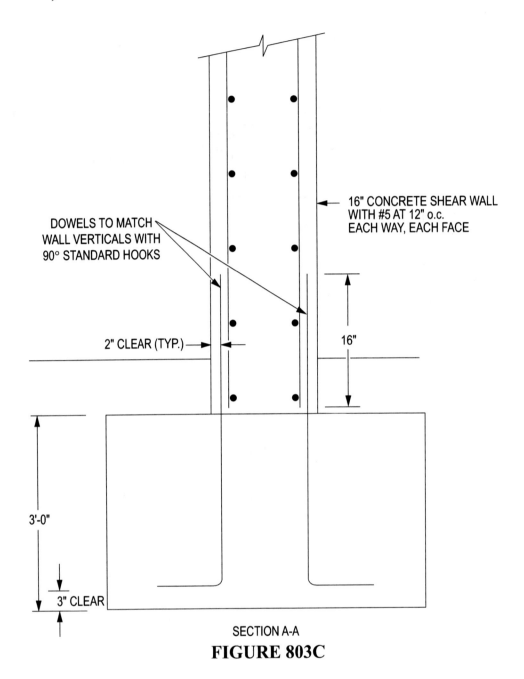

DOWELS TO MATCH WALL VERTICALS WITH 90° STANDARD HOOKS

16" CONCRETE SHEAR WALL WITH #5 AT 12" o.c. EACH WAY, EACH FACE

2" CLEAR (TYP.)

16"

3'-0"

3" CLEAR

SECTION A-A

FIGURE 803C

804. A three-story, wood-framed apartment building is shown in **Figure 804A** and **Figure 804B.** Roof and floor framing are open-web wood trusses spaced 2'-0" o.c. All bearing walls act as shear walls.

Design Codes:

IBC: *International Building Code,* 2012 edition (without supplements).

ASCE 7: *Minimum Design Loads for Buildings and Other Structures,* 2010.

NDS: *National Design Specification for Wood Construction ASD/LRFD,* 2012 edition & *National Design Specification Supplement, Design Values for Wood Construction,* 2012 edition.

NDS: *Special Design Provisions for Wind and Seismic with Commentary,* 2008.

Design Data:

Wood Stud Walls:

Hem-Fir stud grade (plates, studs, and blocking)

2×4 studs with 15/32-in. plywood sheathing on one side only

Wall sheathing nails = 8d commons (0.131 in. diameter $\times$ 2 1/2 in. long)

Plate nails = 16d commons (0.162 in. diameter $\times$ 3 1/2 in. long)

Level	Dead Load (psf)	Live Load (psf)	Snow Load (psf)
Roof	20	–	20
Floor	15	40	–

Assumptions:

Ignore seismic forces.

Dead load of walls is included in floor dead load.

Ignore any influence of the balcony or stairwell.

All open-web wood trusses are top chord bearing.

The wall does not qualify as a perforated shear wall.

REQUIREMENTS:

On the actual exam, any sketches necessary for these requirements must be neatly drawn in your solution pamphlet.

(a) The horizontal service level wind forces at the roof, third floor, and second floor, and the vertical service level wind forces on the roof at Wall Line A are shown in **Figure 804B.** Determine the shear per linear foot and the gross overturning moment for the right-hand-side 10-ft-long shear wall at the second floor on Line A, due to the given service level wind loads.

(b) For the second floor shear wall of **Requirement (a)**, determine all nailing requirements for the sheathing and framing and the net uplift holddown forces.

(c) For the second floor shear wall of **Requirements (a)** and **(b)**, provide a sketch of the wall elevation indicating all required wall elements.

(d) For the cross section indicated in **Figure 804B**, neatly sketch a cross-section detail of the second floor and show the shear transfer connections to the wall below.

804. (Continued)

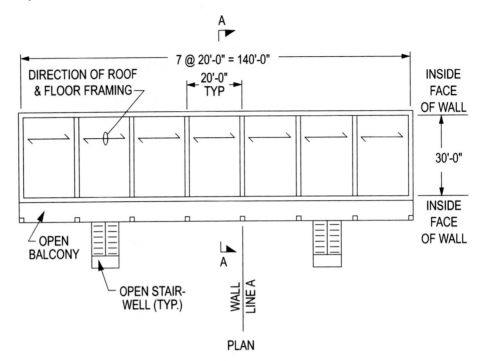

FIGURE 804A

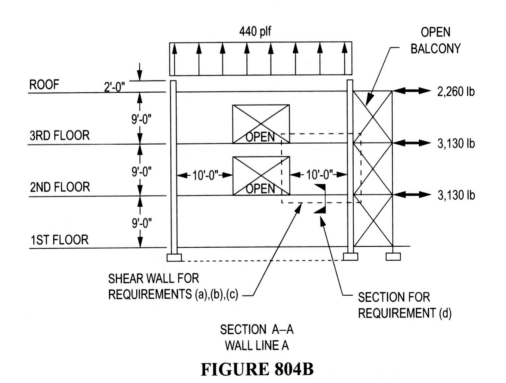

SECTION A–A
WALL LINE A

FIGURE 804B

This completes the afternoon session. Solutions begin on page 207.

LATERAL FORCES PM BRIDGES PRACTICE EXAM

901. **Figure 901A** shows a transverse section of a bridge pier. **Figure 901B** is a column interaction diagram to be used for design of the column. The columns are fixed at the top and bottom in both directions.

Design Specification:
  AASHTO LRFD Bridge Design Specifications, 6th edition, 2012.

Design Data:
  Concrete strength, f'_c 3.5 ksi
  Yield strength of reinforcement, f_y 60 ksi

Factored loads for the Extreme Event I load combination for each column are shown below. Seismic forces have been reduced by the appropriate reduction (R) factor.

  M_u = 4,050 ft-kips
  V_u = 600 kips
  P_u = 2,700 kips (compression)
  Seismic Zone = 4

REQUIREMENTS:

On the actual exam, any sketches necessary for these requirements must be neatly drawn in your solution pamphlet.

(a) For the Extreme Event I load combination, determine the vertical reinforcement required for the column. Neglect any slenderness effect for the column.

(b) For the Extreme Event I load combination, design the required spiral reinforcement.

(c) Sketch an elevation view of the columns showing the size and spacing of the vertical and spiral reinforcements.

901. (Continued)

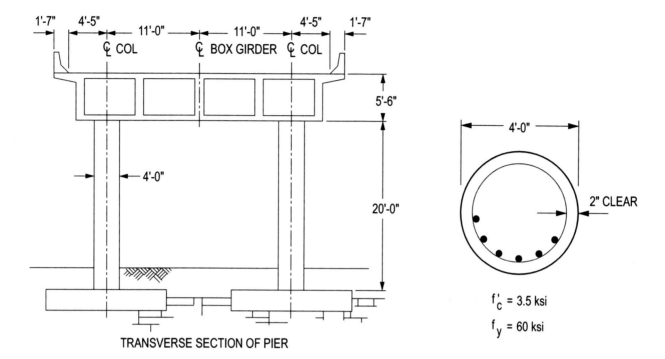

f'_c = 3.5 ksi

f_y = 60 ksi

TRANSVERSE SECTION OF PIER

FIGURE 901A

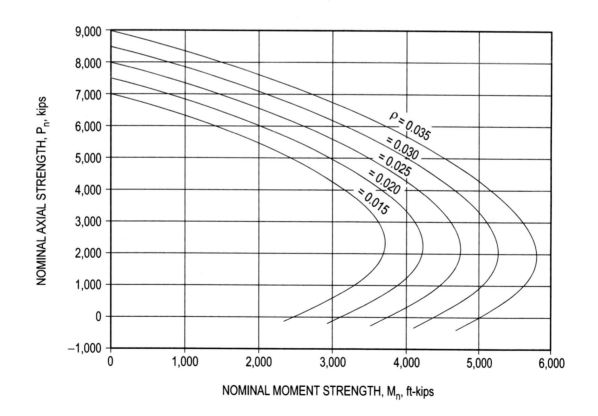

FIGURE 901B

902. **Figure 902A** shows a transverse section of a bridge pier and typical column section. **Figure 902B** is a column interaction diagram for the column. The columns are fixed at the top and bottom in both directions.

Design Specification:
   AASHTO LRFD Bridge Design Specifications, 6th edition, 2012.

Design Data:
Concrete strength, f'_c	4 ksi
Yield strength of reinforcement, f_y	60 ksi (A706, Grade 60)
Nominal bearing resistance of rock	35 ksf

Factored loads at base of each column for the Extreme Event I load combination in the longitudinal direction of the bridge are shown below.

M_u = 4,900 ft-kips
V_u = 650 kips
P_u = 3,000 kips (compression)
Seismic Zone = 4
$\gamma_{EQ} = 0$

Assumptions:
   Ignore column shear forces for footing design.
   Use a response modification factor R of 3.0 for column.
   Ignore weight of footing in all calculations.
   Longitudinal direction controls footing design.
   No soil above footing.

REQUIREMENTS:

On the actual exam, any sketches necessary for these requirements must be neatly drawn in your solution pamphlet.

(a) For the Extreme Event I load combination, determine the footing plan dimension in the longitudinal direction to the nearest foot.

(b) For the Extreme Event I load combination, design the required footing depth and bottom reinforcement (use #10 bars in the longitudinal direction).

902. (Continued)

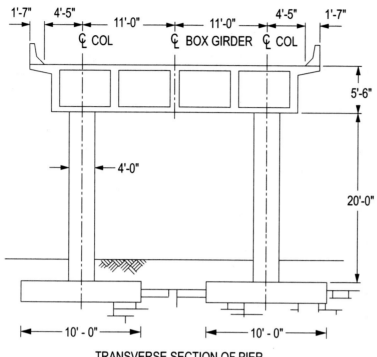

TRANSVERSE SECTION OF PIER

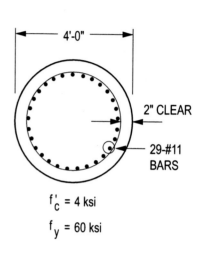

TYPICAL COLUMN SECTION

f'_c = 4 ksi

f_y = 60 ksi

FIGURE 902A

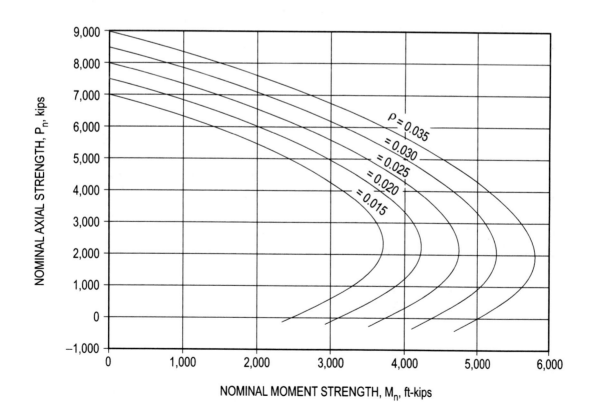

ρ = 0.035

= 0.030

= 0.025

= 0.020

= 0.015

NOMINAL MOMENT STRENGTH, M_n, ft-kips

NOMINAL AXIAL STRENGTH, P_n, kips

FIGURE 902B

903. **Figure 903A** shows the elevation and plan view of a two-span continuous reinforced concrete box girder bridge. The bridge is located in a seismic zone with a peak ground acceleration (PGA) coefficient on rock of 0.55 and with horizontal response spectral acceleration coefficients of 1.4 and 0.58 at the 0.2 sec and 1.0 sec periods, respectively. The substructure is composed of three piers, each with two circular columns fixed at the top and bottom. **Figure 903B** shows the transverse section of the piers. Foundations are directly cast upon hard rock, with $\overline{v}_s > 5,000$ ft/sec.

Design Specification:
   AASHTO LRFD Bridge Design Specifications, 6th edition, 2012.

Design Data:
Concrete strength, f'_c	3.5 ksi
Weight of concrete	0.150 kcf
Yield strength of reinforcement, f_y	60 ksi
Weight of each parapet	0.420 klf
Modulus of elasticity of concrete, E_c	3,403 ksi

The following properties of the box girder have been calculated:
Self-weight, typical voided section	8.77 klf
Distance from bottom fiber to neutral axis	3.00 ft

Assumptions:
   In computing member section properties, gross area of the concrete may be considered.
   For Pier 2, the dead load reactions at the base of the columns have been calculated and are shown in **Figure 903C.** Due to symmetry, there are no moments or shears at the base of the columns of Pier 2 in the longitudinal direction due to dead load.
   Importance category: Other
   $\gamma_{EQ} = 0$

REQUIREMENT:

Determine the maximum factored design forces at the base of the columns of Pier 2 for the Extreme Event I load combination.

Hint: The deflected shape of the superstructure due to a uniform transverse force can be assumed to be a uniform transverse displacement.

903. **(Continued)**

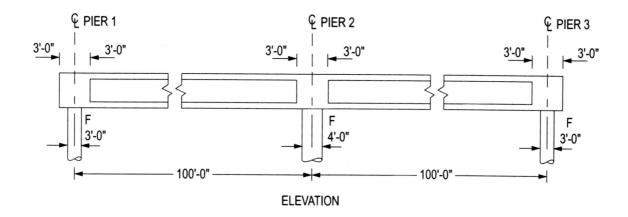

ELEVATION

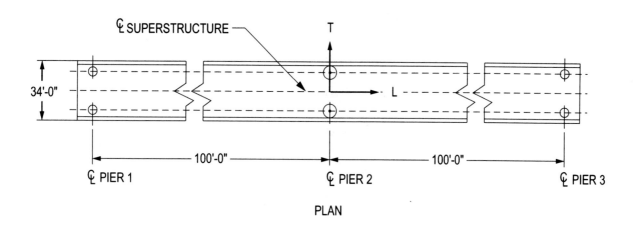

PLAN

FIGURE 903A

185

903. **(Continued)**

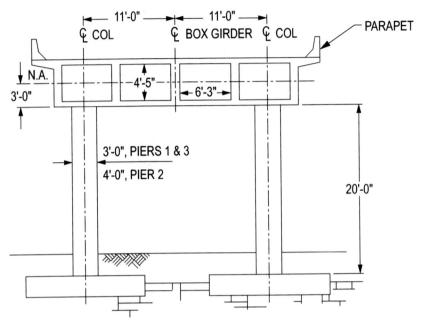

TRANSVERSE SECTION, PIERS 1, 2 AND 3

FIGURE 903B

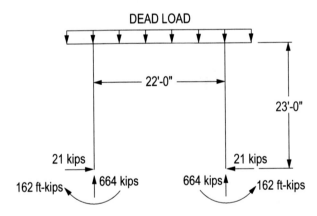

UNFACTORED DEAD LOAD REACTIONS AT PIER 2

FIGURE 903C

This completes the afternoon session. Solutions begin on page 223.

Correct Answers to the AM Lateral Forces Practice Exam

Detailed solutions for each question begin on the next page.

101	C	**121**	A
102	B	**122**	A
103	C	**123**	D
104	B	**124**	C
105	A	**125**	B
106	B	**126**	A
107	B	**127**	B
108	C	**128**	C
109	D	**129**	A
110	B	**130**	C
111	A	**131**	B
112	C	**132**	B
113	C	**133**	A
114	B	**134**	A
115	B	**135**	C
116	A	**136**	B
117	C	**137**	C
118	C	**138**	C
119	C	**139**	B
120	D	**140**	A

101. Not Site Class F or E since no clay, peat, or liquefaction   ASCE 7-10, Section 20.3, and Table 20.3-1

$\bar{v}_s = 1,100$ ft/sec $\therefore$ Site Class D

F_a	$= 1.1$	Table 11.4-1
S_{MS}	$= F_a S_s = (1.1)(1.00) = 1.10$	Eq. 11.4-1
S_{DS}	$= 2/3\, S_{MS} = 0.73$	Eq. 11.4-3
F_v	$= 1.55$	Table 11.4-2
S_{M1}	$= F_v S_1 = (1.55)(0.45) = 0.70$	Eq. 11.4-2
S_{D1}	$= 2/3\, S_{M1} = 0.47$	Eq. 11.4-4
T_0	$= 0.2\, S_{D1}/S_{DS} = 0.13$	Section 11.4.5
T_S	$= S_{D1}/S_{DS} = 0.64$	

Building period $> T_S$ and $< T_L$ $\therefore S_a = \dfrac{S_{D1}}{T} = \dfrac{0.47}{0.80} = 0.58$ Eq. 11.4-6

THE CORRECT ANSWER IS: (C)

---

102. $q_h = 0.00256\, K_h K_{zt} K_d V^2$ ASCE 7-10, Eq. 28.3-1

$h = \dfrac{\left(\dfrac{(4\text{ in.})(30\text{ ft}/2)}{12} + 15\right) + 15}{2} = 17.5$ ft

$K_h = K_{17.5} = 0.875$ Table 28.3-1

$K_{zt} = 1.0$

$K_d = 0.85$ Table 26.6-1

$V = 120$ (Risk Category I - IBC Table 1604.5)

$q_z = 0.00256(0.875)(1.0)(0.85)(120)^2 = 27.4$ psf

THE CORRECT ANSWER IS: (B)

---

103. Force $= \dfrac{(640)(192\text{ ft})}{2} = 61.44$ kips   Note: Load factor = 1.0 for wind for strength design.

Force for one panel $= 30.72$ kips

Number of connectors $= \dfrac{30.72\text{ kips}}{8.5\text{ kips}} = 3.6$;   use 4 connectors

THE CORRECT ANSWER IS: (C)

104.

F_a	$= 1.0$	ASCE 7-10, Table 11.4-1
F_v	$= 1.65$	interpolating from ASCE 7-10, Table 11.4-2
S_{MS}	$= F_a S_s = 1.0(1.0) = 1.0$	ASCE 7-10, Eq. 11.4-1
S_{M1}	$= F_v S_1 = 1.65(0.15) = 0.2475$	ASCE 7-10, Eq. 11.4-2
S_{DS}	$= 2/3\, S_{MS} = 2/3(1.0) = 0.67$	ASCE 7-10, Eq. 11.4-3
S_{D1}	$= 2/3\, S_{M1} = 2/3(0.2475) = 0.165$	ASCE 7-10, Eq. 11.4-4

Determine Seismic Design Category — ASCE 7-10, Table 11.6-1 + Table 11.6-2
IBC Table 1604.5
     Risk Category IV
     S_{DS} is greater than 0.5
     S_{D1} is between 0.133 and 0.20
     $\therefore$ Seismic Design Category is D.
     $I_e = 1.5$ for Risk Category IV — ASCE 7-10, Table 1.5-2

Response Modification factor, R — ASCE 7-10, Table 1.5-2-1
Concentric frame (given) has to be special as ordinary not allowed
over 35 ft in height and structure is $14 + 14 + 12 = 40$ ft tall
$\therefore$ R = 6
Find seismic response coefficient, C_s, used in ASCE 7-10, Eq. 12.8-1

$T = T_a = C_t h_n^x$ — ASCE 7-10, Eq. 12.8-7

$C_t = 0.02$ and $x = 0.75$ (all other structural systems) — ASCE 7-10, Table 12.8-2

$T_a = 0.02(40)^{0.75} = 0.3181$ sec, which is less than T_L

(Eq. 12.8-8 cannot be used as not moment frame structure)

$C_S = \dfrac{S_{DS}}{\left(R/I_e\right)}$ — ASCE 7-10, Eq. 12.8-2

$\quad = \dfrac{0.67}{6/1.5} = 0.1675$ but need not exceed (Eq. 12.8-3) $T < T_L$

$C_S = \dfrac{S_{D1}}{T\left(R/I\right)} = \dfrac{0.165}{0.3181\,(6/1.5)} = 0.1297$

Shall not be less than ASCE 7-10, Eq. 12.8-5

$C_S = 0.044\, S_{DS} I_e \ge 0.01 = 0.044(0.67)(1.5) = 0.044$

$C_S = 0.1$

0.1297 governs

$W = 400 + 600 + 600 = 1{,}600$ kips

Seismic base shear, $V = C_s W = 0.1297(1{,}600) = 208$ kips — ASCE 7-10, Eq. 12.8-1

THE CORRECT ANSWER IS: (B)

105. Uniform load method

$$T = 2\pi\sqrt{\frac{w}{gK}} \quad g = 32.2 \text{ kips/ft}^2$$

$$K = 2\,\text{cols} = 2\left(\frac{12EI}{H^3}\right)$$

$$K\,(2\,\text{cols}) = 2\left[\frac{12 \times 16 \times 10^6}{(21)^3}\right] = 41,464 \text{ kips/ft}$$

$$w = 10 \times 214 = 2,140 \text{ kips}$$

$$T = 2\pi\sqrt{\frac{2,140}{32.2 \times 41,464}} = 0.25 \text{ sec}$$

THE CORRECT ANSWER IS: (A)

106. Per AASHTO Table 3.8.1.2.1-1, the wind load is 50 psf for the direction perpendicular (transverse) to the bridge.

Total wind force at top of the pier for a two-span simply supported bridge:

$$F = \frac{50 \text{ psf}}{1,000} \times (80 \times 2)(7) \times \frac{1}{2}$$

$$= 28 \text{ kips}$$

The unfactored moment at the base of the pier:

$$M = F(h)$$

$$= 28(25 + 3.5)$$

$$= 798 \text{ ft-kips}$$

THE CORRECT ANSWER IS: (B)

107.

$$P_{DL} = (22 + 3)(0.0466) + (4)(8)(0.02)$$

$$= 1.17 + 0.64 = 1.81 \text{ kips}$$

$$M_{DL} = (0.64 \text{ kip})(15 \text{ ft}) = 9.6 \text{ ft-kips}$$

$$M_W = \left[0.6(0.5)(0.060)(25)^2\right] + \left[0.6(4)(8)(0.060)(22)\right] \text{ Note: Load factor = 0.6 for wind for service level.}$$

$$= 11.25 + 25.34 = 36.59 \text{ ft-kips} \qquad \text{Controls}$$

$$f = P/A + M_{max}/S$$

$$= \frac{1.81}{13.7} + \frac{(36.59)(12)}{38.6}$$

$$= 0.13 + 11.375 = 11.51 \text{ ksi}$$

THE CORRECT ANSWER IS: (B)

108. $V = C_S W$ ASCE 7-10, Eq. 12.8-1

$W = (100 \text{ ft})(200 \text{ ft})(15 \text{ psf}) + (2)(200 \text{ ft})(26 \text{ ft} / 2)(70 \text{ psf}) = 664 \text{ kips}$

                        roof   walls

$V = (0.15)(664 \text{ kips}) = 99.6 \text{ kips}$

$\text{Diaphragm chord force} = \dfrac{M}{b}$

$M = \dfrac{wl^2}{8} = \dfrac{(99.6 \text{ kips/200 ft})(200 \text{ ft})^2}{8} = 2,490 \text{ ft-kips}$

$\text{Chord force} = \dfrac{2,490 \text{ ft-kips}}{100 \text{ ft}} = 24.9 \text{ kips}$

THE CORRECT ANSWER IS: (C)

109. Reference: ASCE 7-10, Sections 12.8.4.1 and 12.8.4.2.

Where diaphragms are not flexible, the design shall include the torsional moment due to eccentricity from the center of gravity plus the accidental torsional moment assuming a displacement of 5% of building dimension perpendicular to direction of applied force.

    Accidental $e = 0.05 \times 100 \text{ ft} = 5 \text{ ft}$
    Existing $e = 5 \text{ ft}$
    $T = (75 \text{ kips})(5 \text{ ft} + 5 \text{ ft}) = 750 \text{ ft-kips}$

THE CORRECT ANSWER IS: (D)

110. $V = C_S W$ ASCE 7-10, Eq. 12.8-1

Shear to the left of Member A:

$$W_L = \left[75 \text{ psf} \left(\frac{(17)^2}{2(16)} \right) \times \frac{40}{2} \times 2 \right] + \left[15 \text{ psf} \times 40 \times \frac{40}{2} \right] = 39,094 \text{ lb}$$

$V_L = 0.2 \times 39,094 = 7,818 \text{ lb}$ (for 40-ft diaphragm)

Shear to the right of Member A:

$$W_R = \left[75 \text{ psf} \left(\frac{(17)^2}{2(16)} \right) \times \frac{60}{2} \times 2 \right] + \left[15 \text{ psf} \times 60 \times \frac{60}{2} \right] = 67,641 \text{ lb}$$

$V_R = 0.2 \times 67,641 = 13,528 \text{ lb}$ (for 60-ft diaphragm)

$\text{Drag force} = 7,818 + \left(\dfrac{40}{60} \times 13,528 \right) = 16,837 \text{ lb}$

                (proportion for 40-ft drag strut)

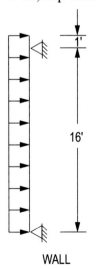

WALL

THE CORRECT ANSWER IS: (B)

111. Check for torsional irregularity $\qquad$ ASCE 7-10, Section 12.3.2.1 + Table 12.3-1

Y Direction: $\quad \Delta_{Y_{AVG}} = \dfrac{\Delta_{FY} + \Delta_{EY}}{2} = \dfrac{0.35 \text{ in.} + 0.25 \text{ in.}}{2} = 0.3 \text{ in.}$

$\qquad \dfrac{\Delta_{FY}}{\Delta_{Y_{AVG}}} = \dfrac{0.35 \text{ in.}}{0.3 \text{ in.}} = 1.17 < 1.2$

X Direction: $\quad \Delta_{X_{AVG}} = \dfrac{\Delta_{BX} + \Delta_{EX}}{2} = \dfrac{0.25 \text{ in.} + 0.5 \text{ in.}}{2} = 0.375 \text{ in.}$

$\qquad \dfrac{\Delta_{EX}}{\Delta_{X_{AVG}}} = \dfrac{0.5 \text{ in.}}{0.375 \text{ in.}} = 1.33 > 1.2$

Building is torsionally irregular.

Check reentrant corner irregularity

$\dfrac{X_{PROJ}}{X_{TOTAL}} = \dfrac{6 \text{ ft}}{50 \text{ ft}} = 0.12 < 0.15$ $\qquad\qquad\qquad$ OK

$\dfrac{Y_{PROJ}}{Y_{TOTAL}} = \dfrac{30 \text{ ft}}{100 \text{ ft}} = 0.3 > 0.15$

No reentrant corner irregularities since both projections are not greater than 15%.

THE CORRECT ANSWER IS: (A)

112.

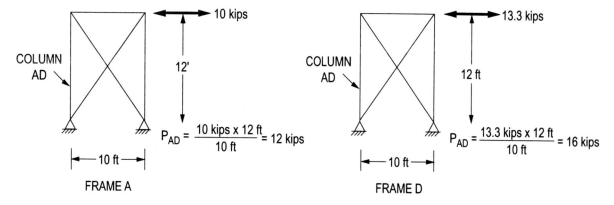

Must combine 100% force + 30% ⊥ force $\qquad$ ASCE 7-10, Sections 12.5.4 and 12.5.3a

$1.0(12) + 0.3(16) = 16.8 \text{ kips}$

$1.0(16) + 0.3(12) = 19.6 \text{ kips}$

Maximum $P_E = 19.6 \text{ kips}$

THE CORRECT ANSWER IS: (C)

113. $w_{wind} = (21\ psf)(1/2)(20\ ft) = 210\ plf$

$$M \quad = \frac{wl^2}{8} = \frac{210(56)^2}{8}$$

$$= 82{,}320\ ft\text{-}lb$$

$$T\ or\ C \quad = \frac{M}{B} = \frac{82.3}{20}$$

$$= 4.12\ kips$$

THE CORRECT ANSWER IS: (C)

114. The shear on each column is 50/2 kips = 25 kips. Assume inflection point is at midheight of column. Moment = 0 at inflection point.

M = 25 kips × 10 ft = 250 ft-kips

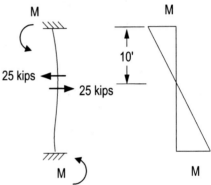

THE CORRECT ANSWER IS: (B)

115. **ASD solution:**

ASD load combinations per ASCE 7-10 Section 2.4

Determine controlling load case.

0.6 D + 0.6 W (uplift)

$$\Sigma M_2 \quad = 0.6(D)(20\ ft)(10\ ft) - 0.6F_W(15\ ft) - R_1(20\ ft) = 0$$

$$0 \quad = 0.6(200\ plf)(20\ ft)(10\ ft) - 0.6F_W(15\ ft) - (-6{,}300\ lb)(20\ ft)$$

$$0.6F = 10.0\ kips$$

115. **(Continued)**

D + 0.6 W

$\Sigma M_2 = (D)(20\,ft)(10\,ft) + 0.6\,F_W\,(15\,ft) - R_1\,(20\,ft) = 0$

$\quad 0 = (200\,plf)(20\,ft)(10\,ft) + (0.6\,F_W)(15\,ft) - (9{,}500\ lb)(20\,ft)$

$0.6\,F_W = 10\ kips$

$\therefore 0.6\,F_W = 10.0$

D + 0.75 (W + L) = D + 0.75 L + 0.75 (0.6 W)

$\Sigma M_2 = (D + 0.75\,L)(20\,ft)(10\,ft) + 0.75\,(0.6\,F_W)(15\,ft) - R_1\,(20\,ft) = 0$

$\quad 0 = \left[200\,plf + 0.75(200\,plf)\right](20\,ft)(10\,ft) + 0.75\,(0.6\,F_W)(15\,ft) - (20\,ft)(R_1) - (9{,}500\ lb)(20\,ft)$

$0.6\,F_W = 10.7\ kips$

LRFD solution:

Determine controlling load case.

0.9 D + 1.0 W (uplift)

$\Sigma M_2 = 0.9(D)(20\,ft)(10\,ft) - (F_W)(15\,ft) - R_1\,(20\,ft) = 0$

$\quad 0 = 0.9(200\,plf)(20\,ft)(10\,ft) - (F_W)(15\,ft) - (-10{,}700\ lb)(20\,ft)$

$F_W = 16.7\ kips \therefore 0.6\,F_W = 10.0\ kips$

1.2 D + 1.0 L + 0.5 W

$\Sigma M_2 = \left[1.2(D) + L\right](20\,ft)(10\,ft) - 0.5\,F_W\,(15\,ft) - R_1\,(20\,ft) = 0$

$\quad 0 = \left[(1.2)(200) + (200)\right](20\,ft)(10\,ft) - 0.5\,F_W\,(15\,ft) - (16{,}900)(20\,ft) = 0$

$F_W = 33.3 \therefore 0.6\ F_W = 20\ kips$

1.2 D + 1.0 L + 1.0 W

$\Sigma M_2 = \left[1.2(D) + L\right](20\,ft)(10\,ft) + F_W\,(15\,ft) - R_1\,(20\,ft) = 0$

$\quad 0 = \left[(1.2)(200) + (200)\right](20\,ft)(10\,ft) + F_W\,(15\,ft) - (16{,}900)(20\,ft) = 0$

$F_W = 16.7\ kips \therefore 0.6\ F_W = 10.0\ kips$

$\therefore 0.6\ F_W = 10.0\ kips$

THE CORRECT ANSWER IS: (B)

116. The ductility of the building is reduced when the amount of reinforcement is increased or when larger-sized bars than those required in the design are used, because the strain in steel reduces as the amount of reinforcement increases.

   THE CORRECT ANSWER IS: (A)

117. Detention facilities are in Risk Category III   IBC Section 308.5 + Table 1604.5

$$\Delta_a = 0.015\, h_{sx}$$
ASCE 7-10 Table 12.12-1

$$h_{sx} = 20\ \text{ft} \times 12 = 240\ \text{in.}$$

$$= 0.015 \times 240\ \text{in.}$$

$$= 3.6\ \text{in.}$$

   THE CORRECT ANSWER IS: (C)

118. Reference: AASHTO LRFD, Table 3.4.1-1 for load combinations and load factors.

   Strength III $1.4\ \text{WS} = 1.4 \times 60\ \text{kips} = 84\ \text{kips}$ Maximum
   Strength V $0.4\ \text{WS} + 1.0\ \text{WL} = 0.4 \times 60 + 1.0 \times 10 = 34\ \text{kips}$

   THE CORRECT ANSWER IS: (C)

119. AASHTO Art. C4.7.4.3.2b

$$\alpha = \int_0^{303} v_s dx = 0.0107\,(303 - 0) = 3.24$$

$$\beta = \int_0^{303} w(x) v_s(x) dx = 8.8 \int_0^{303} v_s(x) dx = 8.8(3.24) = 28.5$$

$$\gamma = \int w(x) v_s(x)^2 dx = 0.0107(28.5) = 0.305$$

$$T = 2\pi \sqrt{\frac{\gamma}{p_o g \alpha}}$$

$$= 2\pi \left[\frac{0.305}{(1.0)(32.2)(3.24)} \right]^{1/2}$$

$$= 0.34\ \text{sec}$$

   THE CORRECT ANSWER IS: (C)

120. The height limit for special reinforced masonry shear walls is 160 ft and does not meet the exception of ASCE, Sec. 12.2.5.4 referenced in Table 12.2-1, Footnote d, which says the height limit may be increased for systems having no irregularities < 60% of lateral force in any line.

THE CORRECT ANSWER IS: (D)

121. The beam is required to resist $R_y F_y A_g$ of one brace in tension and $0.3\,P_n$ of the other in compression.

$R_y = 1.6$

$F_y = 35\ \text{ksi}$

SDM 2nd edition, AISC 341, Sec. F2.3
SDM 2nd edition, AISC 341, Table A3.1
SDM 2nd edition, AISC 341, Table 1-7

A_g of 4 in. $\varnothing$ STD pipe $= 2.96\ \text{in}^2$

$R_y F_y A_g = 1.6(35)(2.96) = 166\ \text{kips}$

Vertical component $= \dfrac{4}{5}(166\ \text{kips}) = 133\ \text{kips}$

Determine $0.3\,P_n$

ASD:

$P_n/\Omega_c = 38.9\ \text{kips for } KL = 12$

AISC, 14th ed., Table 4-6, p. 4-87

$P_n = \left(\dfrac{P_n}{\Omega_c}\right)(\Omega_c) = (38.9)(1.67) = 65.0\ \text{kips}$

LRFD:

$\phi P_n = 58.5\ \text{kips for } KL = 12$

AISC, 14th ed., Table 4-6, p. 4-87

$P_n = \dfrac{\phi P_n}{\phi} = \dfrac{58.5}{0.9} = 65.0\ \text{kips}$

$0.3\,P_n = 0.3(65.0) = 19.5\ \text{kips}$

Vertical component $= \dfrac{4}{5}(19.5) = 15.6\ \text{kips}$

$\therefore$ the vertical portion of the earthquake effect, $E = 133 - 15.6 = 117\ \text{kips}$

THE CORRECT ANSWER IS: (A)

122. The minimum drift angle is 0.02 radian for an intermediate moment frame.

SDM 2nd edition, AISC 341, E2.6b(1)

THE CORRECT ANSWER IS: (A)

123. $K = 2.0$ (Condition f)

$KL = 2L$

AISC 14th ed., Table C-A-7.1

THE CORRECT ANSWER IS: (D)

124. $R_y = 1.4$

$F_y = 46 \text{ ksi}$

SDM 2nd edition, AISC 341, Table A3.1

SDM 2nd edition, AISC 341, Table 1-5b

ASD option:

SDM 2nd edition, AISC 341, Sec. F2.6c(1)

$$\frac{R_y F_y A_g}{1.5} = \frac{(1.4)(46 \text{ ksi})(2.44 \text{ in}^2)}{1.5} = 104.8 \text{ kips}$$

LRFD option:

$$R_y F_y A_g = (1.4)(46 \text{ ksi})(2.44 \text{ in}^2) = 157.1 \text{ kips}$$

THE CORRECT ANSWER IS: (C)

125. $$t_2/t_1 = \frac{0.0566}{0.0566} = 1$$

$\therefore$ Use AISI Eq. E4.3.1-1 to E4.3.1-3

$$P_{ns} = (4.2)\sqrt{(t_2)^3(d)}(F_{u2})$$ Eq. 4.3.1-1

$$= (4.2)\sqrt{(0.0566)^3(0.125)}(62)$$

$$= 1.24$$

$$P_{ns} = (2.7)(t)(d)(F_u)$$ Eq. 4.3.1-2 + 4.3.1-3

$$= (2.7)(0.0566)(0.125)(62)$$

$$= 1.18 \leftarrow \text{controls}$$

ASD:

$$\frac{P_{ns}}{\Omega} = \frac{1.18}{3.00} = 0.393 \text{ kips}$$

$$0.7E = 0.7(2 \text{ kips}) = 1.4 \text{ kips}$$

$$\frac{1.4}{0.393} = 3.56 \rightarrow 4 \text{ screws}$$

LRFD:

$$\phi P_{ns} = (0.5)(1.18) = 0.590 \text{ kips}$$

$$\frac{2.0}{0.590} = 3.39 \rightarrow 4 \text{ screws}$$

THE CORRECT ANSWER IS: (B)

126. R = 740 + 195 = 935 kips   AASHTO 10.6.1.4

$M_T = 39(26 \text{ ft}) = 1,014 \text{ ft-kips}$

$M_L = 16(26 \text{ ft}) = 416 \text{ ft-kips}$

$e_T = \dfrac{1,014}{935} = 1.08 \text{ ft} < L \times \dfrac{0.9}{2} = 12 \times 0.45 = 5.4$ $e_L = \dfrac{416}{935} = 0.44 \text{ ft}$

$e_T / L = \dfrac{1.08}{20} = 0.054 < L \times \dfrac{0.9}{2} = 20 \times 0.45 = 9.0$ $e_L / B = \dfrac{0.44}{12} = 0.037$

$q_{max} = \dfrac{R}{A}\left[1 + 6e_T / L + 6e_L / B\right]$ AASHTO 11.6.3.2 − 2

$q_{max} = \dfrac{935}{(20)(12)}\left[1 + 6(0.054) + 6(0.037)\right]$

$= 6.02 \text{ ksf}$

THE CORRECT ANSWER IS: (A)

127. Weight of 1-ft panel width $= \dfrac{7.25 \text{ in.}}{12}(130 \text{ pcf}) = 78.5 \text{ psf}$

$F_p = 0.4 S_{DS} I_e W_P$ ASCE 7 -10 Sec. 12.11-1

$W_p = \dfrac{W}{2l}(l + a)^2$ (Propped cantilever reaction at diaphragm)

$W_p = \dfrac{78.5 \text{ psf}}{2(23 \text{ ft})}(23 \text{ ft} + 3 \text{ ft})^2 = 1,154 \text{ lb}$

$F_p = 0.4(0.9)(1.0)(1,154) = 415 \text{ plf}$

For 2 ft o.c. (415 plf)(2 ft) = 831 lb

$F_p = 0.4 S_{DS} K_a I_e W_p$ ASCE 7 -10 Sec. 12.11.2.1

Assume $K_a = 2.0$

$F_p = 0.4(0.9)(2.0)(1.0))(1,154) = 831 \text{ plf}$

For 2 ft o.c. (831 plf)(2 ft) = 1,662 lb → controls

THE CORRECT ANSWER IS: (B)

128. $l_{db} = \dfrac{1.25\, A_b f_y}{\sqrt{f'_c}}$ AASHTO 5.11.2.1.1

$= \dfrac{1.25(1.27\text{ in}^2)(60\text{ ksi})}{\sqrt{4\text{ ksi}}} = 47.6\text{ in.}$

but not less than $0.4\, d_b f_y = 0.4\,(1.27\text{ in.})(60\text{ ksi}) = 30.5\text{ in.}$

Modification factor for enclosure within spiral $= 0.75$ AASHTO 5.11.2.1.3

$l_{db} = 48\text{ in.} \times 0.75 = 36\text{ in.}$

For column connections in Seismic Zone 3, increase by 1.25   AASHTO 5.10.11.4.3

$l_{db} = 36\text{ in.} \times 1.25 = 45\text{ in.}$

THE CORRECT ANSWER IS: (C)

129. The correct answer is Details 1 and 2. Detail 3 requires penetrating the formwork (formwork cannot be modified). Detail 4 requires welding at an inaccessible area.

THE CORRECT ANSWER IS: (A)

130. $\sum M_u = -90 + 22.3 + 96.7 + 22.3 = 51.3\text{ ft-kips}$

$V_u = \dfrac{\sum M_u}{L_c} = \dfrac{51.3}{12.0} = 4.28\text{ kips}$

THE CORRECT ANSWER IS: (C)

131. **ASD solution:**

Diaphragm chord force $= \dfrac{M}{b}$

$$M_X = \frac{0.6WX}{2}(l - x) \qquad \text{Note: Load factor = 0.6 for wind for service level}$$

$$M_{@\ 25\ ft} = \frac{(0.6)(333)(25)}{2}(100 - 25) = 187{,}310 \text{ ft-lb}$$

Chord force $= \dfrac{187{,}310 \text{ ft-lb}}{40 \text{ ft}} = 4{,}683 \text{ lb}$

$Z = 100 \text{ lb for 10d common nail}$ NDS Table 11N

$Z' = ZC_D$

$= 100 \text{ lb } (1.6) = 160 \text{ lb}$ NDS Table 2.3.2

Number of nails required $= \dfrac{4{,}683 \text{ lb}}{160 \text{ lb}} = 29.3$

Use 30 10d common nails

LRFD solution:

Diaphragm chord force $= \dfrac{M}{b}$

$$M_{uX} = \frac{WX}{2}(l - x)$$

$$M_{u@\ 25\ ft} = \frac{(333)(25)}{2}(100 - 25) = 312{,}190 \text{ ft-lb}$$

Chord force $= \dfrac{312{,}190 \text{ ft-lb}}{40 \text{ ft}} = 7{,}805 \text{ lb}$

$Z = 100 \text{ lb for 10d common nail}$ NDS Table 11N

$Z' = ZK_F\phi_Z\lambda$

$K_F = 3.32$ NDS Table 10.3-1

$\phi_Z = 0.65$ NDS Table 10.3-1

$Z' = 100(3.32)(0.65)(1.0) = 216 \text{ lb}$

Number of nails required $= \dfrac{7{,}805 \text{ lb}}{216 \text{ lb}} = 36.1$

Use 37 10d common nails

THE CORRECT ANSWER IS: (B)

132. Overturning moment at bottom corner

M = 3 kips(17 ft) + 2 kips(9 ft) − (3 kips + 1 kip + 2 kips + 1 kip)(6 ft) = 27 ft-kips

Tension at holddown

$$T = \frac{27 \text{ ft-kips}}{12 \text{ ft}} \ 2.25 \text{ kips}$$

THE CORRECT ANSWER IS: (B)

133. The best connection for chord/collector is Option (A).

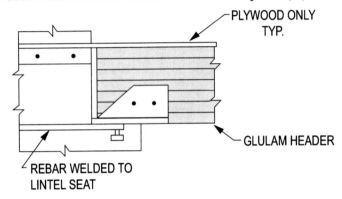

Option (B) has no positive connection at the glulam header.

Option (C) has no chord/collector connection to the tilt-up walls.

Option (D) has wood bolts too close to edge of the glulam header, poor chord/collector connection to the tilt-up walls, and the long row of bolts exacerbates shrinkage cracking/splitting of the glulam header.

THE CORRECT ANSWER IS: (A)

134. $A = 1.5 \text{ in.} \times 12 \text{ in.} \times 2 = 36 \text{ in}^2/\text{ft}$ (use area and inertia of face shells only for ungrouted, un-reinforced cells)

$$I = \frac{(2)(1.5 \text{ in.})^3}{12}(12) + 2(1.5)(12)(11.625/2 - 1.5/2)^2$$
$$= 929.5 \text{ in}^4/\text{ft}$$

$$S = \frac{929.5 \text{ in}^4/\text{ft}}{11.625/2} = 159.9 \text{ in}^3$$

Axial load at midheight

Dead $= 55 \text{ psf} \times 10 \text{ ft} = 550 \text{ plf}$

Seismic $= -0.2 S_{DS} D = -0.2(1.0)(550 \text{ plf}) = -110 \text{ plf}$

$0.6 D + 0.7 E = 0.6(550) + 0.7(-110) = 253 \text{ plf}$

$$f_a = \frac{253}{36} = 7.0 \text{ psi (compression)}$$

Moment at midheight

$$\text{Seismic} = \frac{17 \text{ psf } (20 \text{ ft})^2}{8} = 850 \text{ ft-lb/ft}$$

$0.7 E = 0.7(850) = 595 \text{ ft-lb/ft}$

$$f_b = \frac{595(12)}{159.9} = 44.7 \text{ psi (tension)}$$

Net stress $= 7.0(C) - 44.7(T) = -37.7 \text{ (tension)}$

THE CORRECT ANSWER IS: (A)

135. $P_{roof} = 12 \text{ ft } (15 \text{ psf}) + 0.75[(12 \text{ ft})(40 \text{ psf})] = 540 \text{ plf}$

$$e = \frac{7.625 \text{ in.}}{2} + 3.5 \text{ in.} = 7.31 \text{ in.}$$

$M_{roof} = 540 \text{ plf } (7.31 \text{ in.})/12 \text{ in./ft} = 329 \text{ ft-lb/ft}$

$M_{wind} @ \text{ midheight} = 0.75 [0.6 (33 \text{ psf}) (12 \text{ ft})^2/8] = 270 \text{ ft-lb/ft}$

$M_{midheight \text{ (approximate max)}} = 270 + (329/2) = 435 \text{ ft-lb/ft}$

THE CORRECT ANSWER IS: (C)

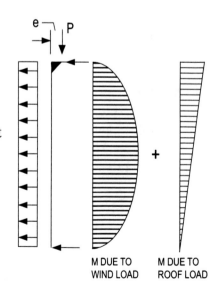

M DUE TO WIND LOAD   M DUE TO ROOF LOAD

136. Seismic Design Category is D based on ASCE 7, Sec. 11.6; therefore must use special reinforced masonry shear walls per ASCE 7, Table 12.2-1.

$R = 5.0$ ASCE 7-2010, Table 12.2-1

$I_e = 1$ ASCE 7-2010, Table 1.5-2

$C_S = \dfrac{S_{DS}}{(R/I_e)} = \dfrac{0.60}{5/1} = 0.120$ ASCE 7-2010, Eq. 12.8-2

THE CORRECT ANSWER IS: (B)

137. Footing area, $A = 2(64) + (24-8)2 = 160 \text{ ft}^2$ $\dfrac{P}{A} = \dfrac{560}{160} = 3.5 \text{ ksf}$

Confirm resultant is within kern $e = \dfrac{M}{P} = \dfrac{2,304 \text{ kips-ft}}{560 \text{ kips}} = 4.11 \text{ ft}$

$B/6 = 32/6 = 5.33 \text{ ft}$

$e < B/6 \;\; \therefore$ resultant within middle 1/3; $\dfrac{P}{A} + \dfrac{M}{S}$ applies

$I = \dfrac{8 \times (24+8)^3}{12} - \dfrac{6 \times 16^3}{12} = 19,797 \text{ ft}^4$

$S = \dfrac{19,797}{16} = 1,237 \text{ ft}^3$

$\dfrac{M}{S} = \dfrac{2,304 \text{ ft-kips}}{1,237 \text{ ft}^3} = 1.9 \text{ ksf}$

Max $f_p = 3.5 + 1.9 = 5.4$

THE CORRECT ANSWER IS: (C)

138. Pile Cap A
        $1.2 \, D + 1.6 \, L = 1.2(200) + 1.6(300) = 720 \text{ kips}$
Pile Cap B
        $1.2 \, D + 1.6 \, L = 1.2(280) + 1.6(520) = 1,168 \text{ kips}$
Seismic tie tension or compression   IBC 2012, Sec. 1810.3.13

$T = C = \dfrac{1.2 \, D \times S_{DS}}{10} = \dfrac{1.2(280)(0.75)}{10} = 25.2 \text{ kips}$

$T = C = 0.25 \times 1.2 \, D = 0.25(1.2)(200) = 60.0 \text{ kips}$

$\therefore \; T = C = 25.2 \text{ kips}$

THE CORRECT ANSWER IS: (C)

139. 50 psf   AASHTO Table 3.8.1.2.1-1

$$P = (50 \text{ psf})(7.083 \text{ ft})(70 \text{ ft})\left(\frac{1}{1,000}\right) = 24.79 \text{ kips}$$

$$M(\text{wind on superstructure}) = (24.79 \text{ kips})(6.54 \text{ ft}) = 162.1 \text{ ft-kips}$$

$$\text{Axial load on exterior pile} = \frac{162.1 \text{ kips}}{2(11.0)} = 7.4 \text{ kips}$$

distance between exterior piles

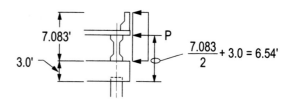

THE CORRECT ANSWER IS: (B)

140. IBC Section 1704.5.1 states that a structure with a height greater than 75 ft requires structural observations for seismic resistance.

THE CORRECT ANSWER IS: (A)

LATERAL FORCES PM BUILDINGS SOLUTIONS

801. **(a) Items at exterior CMU wall:**

1. Adequacy of CMU parapet for wind and seismic out-of-plane loads.
2. Adequacy of CMU wall for combined loading of vertical loads with wind and seismic out-of-plane loads.
3. Adequacy of CMU wall for wind and seismic in-plane loads (shear walls).

Items at roof framing:

1. Out-of-plane anchorage for exterior CMU wall.
2. Adequacy of wood sheathing diaphragm for wind and seismic loads.
3. In-plane connection to exterior CMU wall for transfer of diaphragm forces.
4. Adequacy of struts and chords of diaphragm.
5. Uplift connection to exterior CMU wall for transfer of wind forces.

Items at foundation system:

1. Adequate safety factor for overturning.
2. Adequate safety factor for sliding.
3. Adequate safety factor for uplift.
4. Adequacy of soil bearing pressure.
5. Adequacy of connection to CMU wall.

(b) Design wind pressure on the parapet   ASCE 7, Sec. 30.9

$p = q_p (GC_p - GC_{pi})$ (Components and cladding elements of parapets)

$q_p = 0.00256\, K_z K_{zt} K_d V^2$ ASCE 7, Eq. (30.3-1)

$K_z = 0.90$ Exposure C, $z = 20$ ft (top of parapet)   ASCE 7, Table 30.3-1

$K_{zt} = 1.67$ (given)

$K_d = 0.85$ ASCE 7, Table 26.6-1

$V = 142$ mph (given)

$q_p = 0.00256 \times 0.90 \times 1.67 \times 0.85 \times 142^2 = 65.9$ psf

$GC_{pi} = 0.00$ (solid parapet, open building condition)   ASCE 7, Table 26.11-1

GC_p, $h \leq 60$ ft   ASCE 7, Fig. 30.4-1

Effective wind area   ASCE 7, Sec. 26.2

  = span length 4-ft height × span 4 ft/3 = 16/3 = 5.3 ft^2 < 10 ft^2 Use 10 ft^2

Zone 4 wall positive pressure $GC_p = +1.0 \times 0.90 = +0.90$ (Ref footnote 5 for reduction)

Zone 4 wall negative pressure $GC_p = -1.1 \times 0.90 = -0.99$ (Ref footnote 5 for reduction)

Zone 2 roof negative pressure $GC_p = -1.8$ ASCE 7 Fig. 30.4-2A

ASCE 7 FIGURE 30.9-1

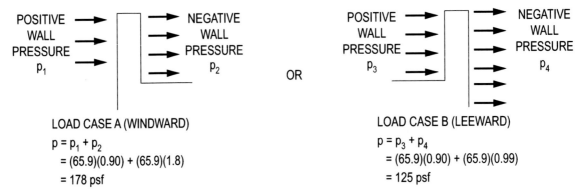

LOAD CASE A (WINDWARD)

$p = p_1 + p_2$

 = (65.9)(0.90) + (65.9)(1.8)

 = 178 psf

LOAD CASE B (LEEWARD)

$p = p_3 + p_4$

 = (65.9)(0.90) + (65.9)(0.99)

 = 125 psf

801. (Continued)

Seismic design force on the parapet: ASCE 7, Sec. 13.3.1

$$F_p = \frac{0.4\, a_p\, S_{DS}\, W_p}{(R_P / I_P)}\left(1 + 2\frac{z}{h}\right)$$ ASCE 7, Eq. (13.3-1)

where $\dfrac{z}{h} = \dfrac{16'}{16'}$ $I_p = 1.0$ ASCE 7, Sec 13.1.3

$a_p = 2.5;$ $R_p = 2.5$ (parapets–unbraced)   ASCE 7, Table 13.5.1

$$F_p = \frac{0.4 \times 2.5 \times 0.70 \times 60}{\left(\dfrac{2.5}{1.0}\right)}\,(1+2) = 50\text{ psf}$$

Controlling design load on the parapet = 178 psf (windward pressure)

(c) Check if the existing #5 @ 48" o.c. vertical at centerline of wall is adequate for the parapet:

$V_{max} = 100\text{ psf } (1')(4') = 400\text{ lb}/\text{ft wall}$

$$M_{max} = \frac{100\text{ psf }(1')(4')^2}{2} = 800\text{ ft-lb}/\text{ft wall}$$

Check shear stress:
Since no shear reinforcement is provided, assume one face shell resists shear force.

$$f_v = \frac{3V}{2A} = \frac{3(400)}{2(1\,1/4")(12")} = 40\text{ psi}$$

F_v shall not exceed: TMS 402 Sec 2.2.5.2

(a) $1.5\sqrt{f'_m} = 1.5\sqrt{1,500} = 58$ psi

(b) 120 psi

(c) $37\text{ psi} + 0.45\, N_v / A_n$

   $= 37 + 0.45\,(180 + 240)/A_n$

A_n based on two face shells and one grouted cell per 48"

$$A_n = \frac{(2)(1\,1/4")(48") + (6"+1"+1\,1/4")(7\,5/8"-(2)1\,1/4")}{4\text{ ft}}$$

$A_n = 40.6\text{ in}^2/\text{ft}$

   $= 37 + 0.45\,(420)/40.6 = 41.7$ psi

$\therefore F_v = 41.7\text{ psi} > f_v = 40\text{ psi}$ OK

209

801. (Continued)

Check flexural capacity:

$$A_s = 0.31 \, in^2 \, (12/48) = 0.0775 \, in^2 \, / \, ft$$

$$\rho = \frac{0.0775}{(12)(7.625/2)} = 0.0017$$

$$\eta = \frac{E_s}{E_m} = \frac{29 \times 10^6}{900 \, (1,500)} = 21.48$$

$$\eta\rho = (21.48)(0.0017) = 0.037$$

$$k = \sqrt{\eta\rho^2 + 2\eta\rho} - \eta\rho = 0.238$$

$$j = 1 - k/3 = 0.921$$

$$f_b = \frac{2\,m}{kjbd^2} = \frac{(2)(800)(12)}{(0.238)(0.921)(12)(7.625/2)^2} = 502 \, psi$$

$$F_b = 0.45 \, f'_m = 0.45(1,500) = 675 \, psi \qquad \text{TMS 402 Sec 2.3.4.2.2}$$

$$F_b > f_b \qquad OK$$

$$f_s = \frac{m}{A_s jd} = \frac{(800)(12)}{(0.0775)(0.921)(7.625/2)} = 35,278 \, psi$$

$$F_s = 32,000 \, psi \qquad \text{TMS 402 Sec 2.3.3.1(b)}$$

$$F_s < f_s \qquad \text{No good}$$

$\therefore$ #5 @ 48" o.c. in 8" CMU parapet wall (partially grouted) is inadequate.

801.   **(Continued)**

(d) The roof diaphragm requires attachment to the existing masonry wall for an out-of-plane anchorage force of 420 plf. Provide a sketch for a complete wall anchorage connection at 48" o.c. Identify all required components, but do not design.

Steel elements of wall anchorage are designed for 1.4× forces per ASCE 12.11.2.2.2.

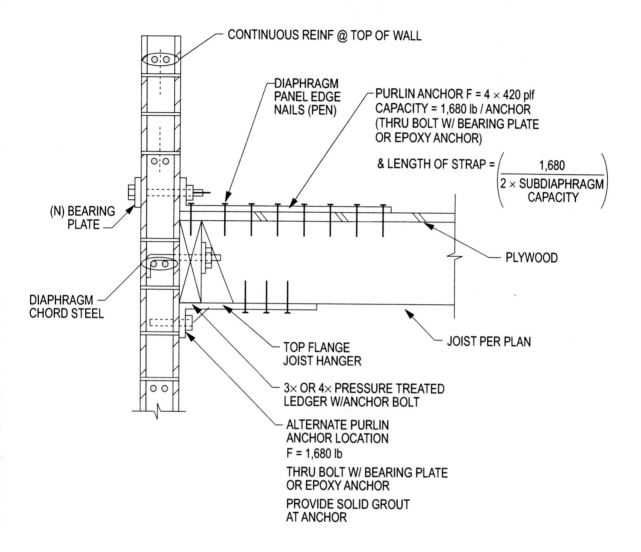

802. **(a) Force in braced frame**

The problem assumptions state that all frames have the same rigidity.

- Direct shear in east-west direction:
The frames on Grid Lines 2 and 4 each take half of the direct shear, or 75 kips each. Direct shear in frames on Grid Lines A and E is zero.

- Center of mass (CM)
Assume the center of mass is at the center of the floor diaphragm midway between Grid Lines 2 and 3 and centered on Grid Line C.

- Center of rigidity (CR)
The center of rigidity is at the intersection of Grid Line 3 and Grid Line C. From an origin point at Grid Lines 4 and A, $x = 80$ ft and $y = 80$ ft.
Accidental torsion, $e = 0.05 \times 122 = 6.1$ ft.

- Torsional moment
The maximum torsional moment MT is the story force acting at a moment arm of $[(CR - CM) + e]$
$M_T = 150 \times [(80' - 60') + 6.1] = 3,915$ ft-kips

- Polar moment of inertia
$J = \sum r^2 R$ with R constant so assume $R = 1$
$J = \sum r^2 = 2[(1 \times 80^2) + (1 \times 40^2)]$
$\quad = 16,000$

- Horizontal distribution of story shears
$$V_2 = 75 + \frac{3,915 \times 40}{16,000} = 84.8 \text{ kips}$$

(b) Design of Brace 2

Frame is a SCBF in Seismic Design Category D.

- Unfactored seismic force in Brace 2 (Strength Level):

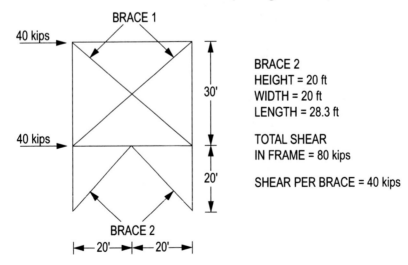

$$Q_E = \text{brace force} = 40 \times \frac{28.3}{20} = 56.6 \text{ kips (tension or compression)}$$

Design and detail of brace to meet requirements of AISC *Seismic Design Manual* (SDM).

802. **(Continued)**

Slenderness limit $\dfrac{KL}{r} \leq 200$ $\qquad$ SDM 341 Sec. F2.5b

Use K = 1.0

$r \geq \dfrac{KL}{200} \geq \dfrac{1.0(28.3)(12)}{200} \geq 1.70$

Limiting width to thickness ratio for brace (highly ductile member)

$\qquad$ D/t $\leq$ 0.038 E/f$_y$ $\qquad$ SDM 341 Sec. F2.5a and Table D1.1

Pipe A53 Grade B, f$_y$ = 35 ksi

$0.038 \times \dfrac{29,000}{35} = 31.5$

SDM Table 1-7 lists pipe sections that satisfy local buckling requirements

- Required strength
  1. Compression 1.2 D + 1.0 E + 0.5 L $\qquad$ IBC Eq. (16-5)
     where $\qquad$ ASCE 7 Sec 2.3.2 (Eq.5)
     $\qquad$ E = ρ Q$_E$ + 0.2 S$_{DS}$D

     Problem statement says that braces do not carry any gravity loads.
     Therefore D = L = 0 and vertical seismic term 0.2 S$_{DS}$D = 0

     P$_u$ = ρ Q$_E$ = 1.0 × 56.6 = 56.6 kips
     KL = 1.0 × 28.3 = 28.3 ft

     AISC Tables 1-14 and 4-6:
     Try: 8" diameter standard weight (std.) KL = 29 ft
     $\qquad$ ϕ_c P$_c$ = 121 kips > P$_u$ = 56.6 kips
     $\qquad$ D/t = 28.8 < 31.5 $\qquad$ OK
     $\qquad$ r = 2.95 > 1.70 $\qquad$ OK
     $\qquad$ 8" standard pipe OK for compression

  2. Tension 0.9 D + 1.0 E $\qquad$ IBC Eq. (16-7)
     T$_u$ = ρ Q$_E$ = 56.6 kips $\qquad$ ASCE 7 Sec 2.3.2 (Eq.7)

     AISC Table 5-7:
     Yielding on gross section (no net reduction in section)
     $\qquad$ ϕ_t P$_n$ = 247 kips

Assume no reduction in net section or section is reinforced so that the effective net section is at least as great as the brace cross section. This is to avoid net section fracture (SDM 341 commentary section F2.5b)

802. (Continued)

Note: If unreinforced slotted gusset connection is used, the required tensile strength shall be greater than the lesser of:

$T_u = R_y F_y A_g < \phi R_t F_u A_e$

or

Maximum load effect, indicated by analysis that can be transferred to the brace to the system.

∴ Provide reinforcement plates where the section is reduced at the slot for the gusset plate.

Provide 8" diameter standard pipe brace.

(c) Sketch of Brace 2 to Column B-2 connection.

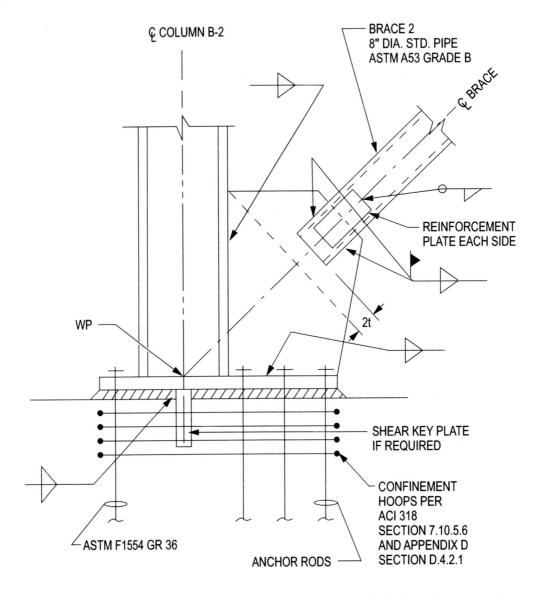

₵ COLUMN B-2

BRACE 2
8" DIA. STD. PIPE
ASTM A53 GRADE B

₵ BRACE

REINFORCEMENT
PLATE EACH SIDE

2t

WP

SHEAR KEY PLATE
IF REQUIRED

CONFINEMENT
HOOPS PER
ACI 318
SECTION 7.10.5.6
AND APPENDIX D
SECTION D.4.2.1

ASTM F1554 GR 36

ANCHOR RODS

t = GUSSET PLATE THICKNESS

803. (a) Seismic base shear

$F_a = 1.38$ for Site Class D and $S_S = 0.52$ · · · · · · · · · · · · · · ASCE 7 Table 11.4-1

$S_{MS} = F_a S_s = 1.38 \times 0.52 = 0.72$ · · · · · · · · · · · · · · · ASCE 7 Eq. (11.4-1)

$S_{DS} = 2/3\, S_{MS} = 2/3 \times 0.72 = 0.48$ · · · · · · · · · · · · · · ASCE 7 Eq. (11.4-3)

$\therefore$ Seismic Design Category = C · ASCE 7 Table 11.6-1

$F_v = 2.08$ for Site Class D and $S_1 = 0.18$ · · · · · · · · · · · · · · · ASCE 7 Table 11.4-2

$S_{M1} = F_v S_1 = 2.08 \times 0.18 = 0.37$ · · · · · · · · · · · · · · · · ASCE 7 Eq. (11.4-2)

$S_{D1} = 2/3\, S_{M1} = 2/3 \times 0.37 = 0.25$ · · · · · · · · · · · · · · · ASCE 7 Eq. (11.4-4)

$\therefore$ Seismic Design Category = D · ASCE 7 Table 11.6-2

Most severe seismic design category controls, so building is Seismic Design Category D

$V = C_s W$ · ASCE 7, Eq. (12.8-1)

Seismic weight, W = 2,510 kips (given)

$$C_s = \frac{S_{DS}}{(R/I)}$$ · ASCE 7, Eq. (12.8-2)

$I_e = 1.0$ (given)

Considering the seismic force resisting system of the building as building frame system Type B4 special reinforced concrete shear wall. · · · · · · · · · · ASCE 7 Table 12.2-1

$R = 6 \qquad \Omega = 2.5 \qquad C_d = 5$

$$C_s = \frac{S_{DS}}{(R/I)} = \frac{0.48}{6/1.0} = 0.080$$

(Alternatively, consider as bearing wall system Type A1 special reinforced concrete shear wall, as wall locations are also bearing. Use R = 5, which is conservative but not unreasonable.)

$T = T_a = C_t h_n^x = 0.020(45)^{0.75} = 0.35$ sec. · · · ASCE 7 Eq. (12.8-7) and Table 12.8-2

$T < T_L$ given

$$C_{s\,max} = \frac{S_{D1}}{T(R/I)} = \frac{0.25}{0.35(6/1.0)} = 0.119$$ · · · · · · · ASCE 7 Eq. (12.8-3)

$C_{s\,min} = 0.044\, S_{DS} I_e \geq 0.01$ · · · · · · · · · · · · · · · · · ASCE 7 Eq. (12.8-5)

$= 0.044 \times 0.48 \times 1.0 = 0.02$

$\therefore C_s = 0.080$

$V = C_s W = 0.080 \times 2,510 = 201$ kips

803. **(Continued)**

(b) Seismic story forces

Vertical distribution of seismic forces:

$$F_x = C_{vx}V$$ ASCE 7 Eq. (12.8-11)

$$C_{vx} = \frac{w_x h_x^k}{\sum w_i h_i^k}$$ ASCE 7 Eq. (12.8-12)

$V_{base} = 201$ kips from **Requirement (a).**

Distribute forces vertically.

Level	w_i, kips (given)	h_i, ft (given)	$w_i h_i$	$\dfrac{w_i h_i}{\sum w_i h_i}$	V_i, kips
Roof	550	45	24,750	0.36	72.4
3rd	980	30	29,400	0.43	86.4
2nd	980	15	14,700	0.21	42.2
Σ	2,510		68,850	1.0	201

$F_{roof} = 72.4$ kips

$F_{3rd} = 86.4$ kips

$F_{2nd} = 42.2$ kips

(c) Check (2) #5 @ 12" o.c.

Shear Friction: ACI Sec 11.6.4

$$\phi V_n = \phi A_{vf} f_y \mu$$ ACI Eq. (11-25)

$$A_{vf} = \frac{2 \times 0.31}{1.0 \text{ ft}} = 0.62 \text{ in}^2/\text{ft}$$

$f_y = 60$ ksi (given)

$\phi = 0.6$ ACI Sec 9.3.4(a)

$\mu = 0.60\lambda$ (No information is given about surface of foundation) ACI Sec. 11.6.4.3

$\lambda = 1.0$ Normal weight concrete

$\phi V_n = 0.6 \times 0.62 \times 60 \times (0.60 \times 1.0) = 13.4$ kips/ft

Max $\phi V_n = \phi\, 0.2 f'_c A_c = (0.6)(0.2)(3)(16)(12) = 69.1$ kips/ft ACI Sec 11.6.5

Max $\phi V_n = \phi\, 800 A_c = 0.6 \times 800 \times 16 \times 12/1,000 = 92.2$ kips

$\therefore \phi V_n = 13.4$ kips/ft > 6.0 kips/ft OK

NOTE: If there is tension across the joint, additional reinforcing steel is required.

803. **(Continued)**

Hooked dowel embedment:

$$\ell_{dh} = \frac{0.02 \, \psi_e f_y}{\lambda \sqrt{f_c'}} d_b \qquad \text{ACI Sec. 12.5.2}$$

$$= \frac{0.02(1.0)(60,000)}{1.0\sqrt{3,000}}(5/8) = 21.9"$$

$\ell_{dh} = 21.9" < 33"$ provided   OK

Splice of vertical bars :

Assume class B splice required   ACI Sec. 12.15.2

Class B splice $= 1.3 \, \ell_d$ ACI Sec. 12.15.1

$$\ell_d = \left(\frac{f_y \, \psi_t \psi_e}{25 \, \lambda \sqrt{f_c'}} \right) d_b \qquad \text{ACI Sec. 12.2.2}$$

$$= \frac{(60,000)(1.0)(1.0)}{(25)(1.0)(\sqrt{5,000})}(5/8) = 21.2" \qquad \text{ACI Sec. 12.2.2}$$

Class B splice $= 1.3(21.2) = 27.6"$

$27.6" > 16"$ provided

$\therefore$ Dowels are not adequate

(d) Check horizontal wall reinforcement

$V_u = 6.0$ kips/ft

$$\phi V_n = \phi \, A_{cv} \left(\alpha_c \lambda \sqrt{f_c'} + \rho_t f_y \right) \qquad \text{ACI Eq. (21-7)}$$

$h_w = 45$ ft $l_w = 30$ ft $h_w / l_w = 1.5$ $\therefore$ $\alpha_c = 3.0$

$\phi = 0.60$ ACI Sec 9.3.4

$\rho_t = \dfrac{2 \times 0.31}{12 \times 16} = 0.0032 \geq 0.0025 \therefore$ meets minimum   ACI Sec 21.9.2.1

$A_{cv} = 12 \times 16 = 192 \text{ in}^2$

$$\phi V_n = 0.60 \times 192 \times \left[(3.0)(1.0)\sqrt{5,000} + (0.0032)(60,000) \right] \left(\frac{1}{1,000} \right)$$

$\phi V_n = 46.6$ klf $\geq V_u \left(= 6.0 \text{ klf} \right) \therefore$ OK

(e) Possible repair solution

Calculate adequacy of development of straight dowels, and provide additional dowels (drilled and epoxied) if required

217

804. **(a) Wind force at top of shear wall:**

$$V = \frac{2{,}260 \text{ lb}}{2} + \frac{3{,}130 \text{ lb}}{2} = 2{,}695 \text{ lb}$$

Shear per linear foot of shear wall:

$$V = \frac{2{,}695 \text{ lb}}{10 \text{ ft}} = 270 \text{ plf}$$

Gross overturning moment at shear wall:

$$M_{gross} = \left(\frac{2{,}260}{2}\right)(18) + \left(\frac{3{,}130}{2}\right)(9) + (440)(10)\left(\frac{10}{2}\right)$$

$$= 56{,}425 \text{ ft-lb}$$

(b) Nailing requirements of shear wall: NDS SDPWS Table 4.3A

15/32" wood structural panels-sheathing
w/ 8d nails @ 6" o.c. @ panel edges
and @ 12" o.c. @ intermediate supports, $V_w = 730$ plf
Footnote 3 specific adjustment factor:
$= [1 - (0.5 - G)]$
Hem-Fir $G = 0.43$ NDS Table 11.3.3A
$= [1 - (0.5 - 0.43)] = 0.93$

$$V_{Allow} = \frac{730 \text{ plf}}{2.0} \times 0.93 = 340 \text{ plf} > 270 \text{ plf} \quad \text{OK}$$

Bottom plate to blocking between trusses   NDS Table 11N:
For 16d nails and 2×4 bottom plate ($t_s = 1\ 1/2$")
$Z = 122$ lb
Penetration into main member (blocking):
$p = 3\ 1/2 - 1\ 1/2 - 3/4 = 1\ 1/4$"

$6\,D = 6\ (0.162) = 0.972$"

$10\,D = 10(0.162) = 1.62$"

$\therefore 6\,D < p < 10\,d \rightarrow$ use adj. factor footnote 3

$z' = 122 \text{ lb} \times C_D \times p / 10\,d$

$\quad = 122 \times 1.6 \times 1.25 / 1.62 = 150 \text{ lb} / \text{nail}$

$$\text{Required spacing} = \frac{150}{270} = 0.56' = 6.7"$$

$\therefore$ Attach bottom plate to blocking with 16d nails @ 6" o.c. (max.)

804. **(Continued)**

Blocking between trusses to top plate (wall below)
Use 16d toe nails

NDS Table 11N:

$z = 122$ lb (from above)

Penetration of toe nail into main member (top plate):

$$p = \ell \cos 30° - \ell/3 = 3\,1/2\,(\cos 30°) - \frac{3\,1/2}{3} = 1.86"$$

$$\therefore p > 10\,d$$

$$z' = 122\,\text{lb} \times C_D \times C_{tn}$$

$$= 122 \times 1.6 \times 0.83 = 162\,\text{lb/nail}$$

$$\text{Required spacing} = \frac{162}{270} = 0.6' = 7.2"$$

$\therefore$ Attach blocking to top plate with 16d toe nails @ 7" o.c. max.

Alternately, provide metal framing clips from blocking to top plate with correct combination of capacity and spacing for overall resistance of 270 plf

Net uplift holdown forces:

At location adjacent to balcony:

$M_{gross} = 56,425$ ft-lb (from requirement (a))

$$M_{0.6\,D} = 0.6(20\,\text{psf})(20\,\text{ft})(10\,\text{ft})(10\,\text{ft}/2)$$

$$+ 0.6(15\,\text{psf})(20\,\text{ft})(10\text{-ft})(10\,\text{ft}/2) = 21,000\,\text{ft-lb}$$

$$M_{net} = 56,425 - 21,000 = 35,425\,\text{ft-lb}$$

$$T_{@holdown} = \frac{M}{b} = \frac{35,425\,\text{ft-lb}}{10'} = 3,543\,\text{lb}$$

At location adjacent to 10-ft opening:

$$T_{@\,holdown} = T_{shear\,wall} + T_{header}$$

$$T_{header} = 440\,\text{plf}\,(10\,\text{ft}/2) - 0.6(20\,\text{psf} + 15\,\text{psf})(20\,\text{ft})\,(10\,\text{ft}/2) = 100\,\text{lb}$$

$$\therefore T_{@\,holdown} = 3,543 + 100 = 3,643\,\text{lb}$$

804. **(Continued)**
   (c) Shear wall elevation sketch

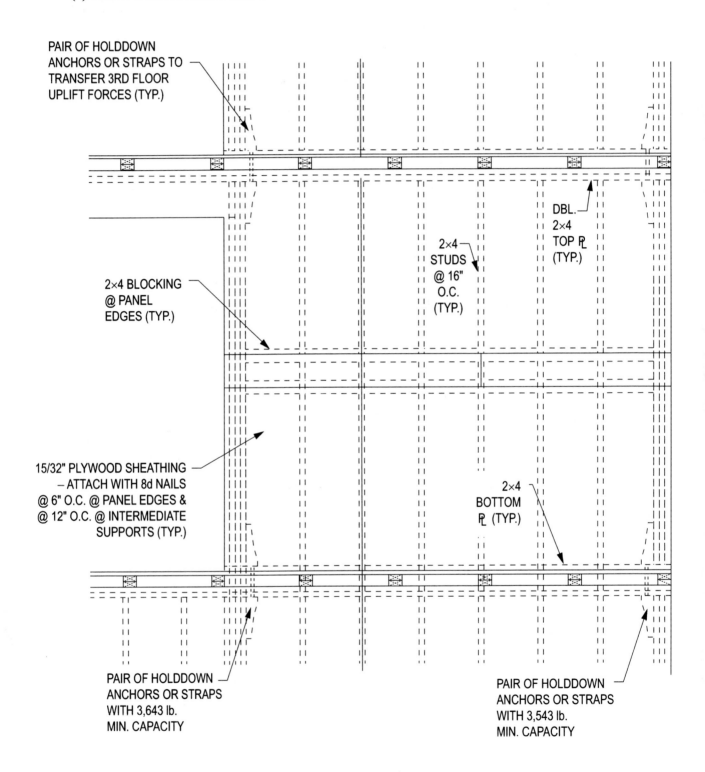

PAIR OF HOLDDOWN
ANCHORS OR STRAPS TO
TRANSFER 3RD FLOOR
UPLIFT FORCES (TYP.)

DBL.
2×4
TOP PL
(TYP.)

2×4
STUDS
@ 16"
O.C.
(TYP.)

2×4 BLOCKING
@ PANEL
EDGES (TYP.)

15/32" PLYWOOD SHEATHING
– ATTACH WITH 8d NAILS
@ 6" O.C. @ PANEL EDGES &
@ 12" O.C. @ INTERMEDIATE
SUPPORTS (TYP.)

2×4
BOTTOM
PL (TYP.)

PAIR OF HOLDDOWN
ANCHORS OR STRAPS
WITH 3,643 lb.
MIN. CAPACITY

PAIR OF HOLDDOWN
ANCHORS OR STRAPS
WITH 3,543 lb.
MIN. CAPACITY

804. (Continued)
(d) Cross section at shear wall

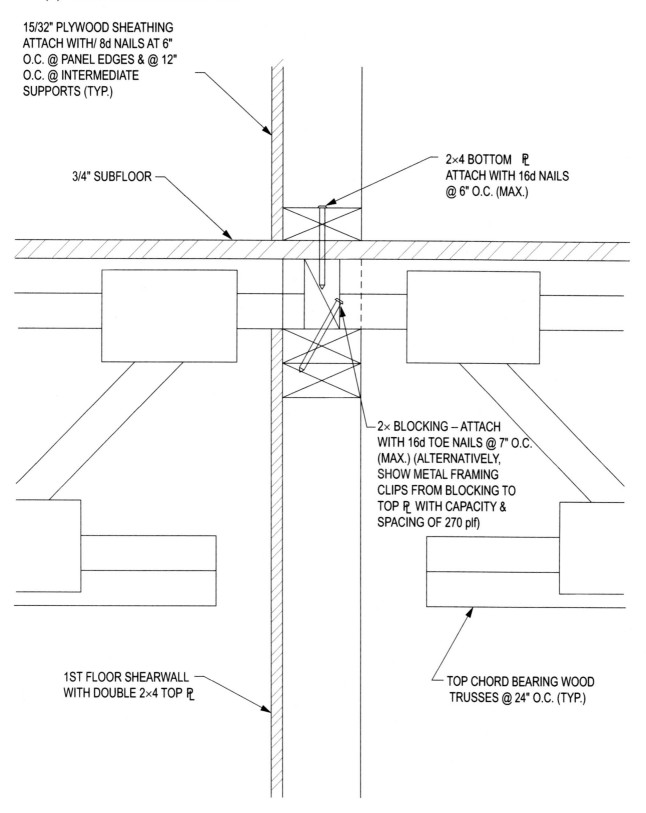

15/32" PLYWOOD SHEATHING
ATTACH WITH/ 8d NAILS AT 6"
O.C. @ PANEL EDGES & @ 12"
O.C. @ INTERMEDIATE
SUPPORTS (TYP.)

3/4" SUBFLOOR

2×4 BOTTOM ℄
ATTACH WITH 16d NAILS
@ 6" O.C. (MAX.)

2× BLOCKING – ATTACH
WITH 16d TOE NAILS @ 7" O.C.
(MAX.) (ALTERNATIVELY,
SHOW METAL FRAMING
CLIPS FROM BLOCKING TO
TOP ℄ WITH CAPACITY &
SPACING OF 270 plf)

1ST FLOOR SHEARWALL
WITH DOUBLE 2×4 TOP ℄

TOP CHORD BEARING WOOD
TRUSSES @ 24" O.C. (TYP.)

901. (a) Vertical reinforcement required for the column

Design for moment and axial force

Column requirement, Art. 5.10.11.4.1

h/D_c = ratio of clear height to maximum plan dimension of column
= 20/4 = 5 > 2.5

The column qualifies to be designed as a column and not as a pier.

Slenderness of the column, Art. 5.7.4.3, may be ignored per problem statement.

Vertical reinforcement, flexural strength, Art. 5.10.11.4.1b

Design for M_u = 4,050 ft-kips and $P_{u\,max}$ = 2,700 kips

ϕ = 0.9

M_n = nominal moment $= M_u/\phi$ = 4,050/0.9 = 4,500 ft-kips

P_n = nominal axial force $= P_u/\phi$ = 2,700/0.9 = 3,000 kips

From the interaction diagram for M_n = 4,500 ft-kips and P_n = 3,000 kips

ρ = 0.025

Limits of vertical reinforcement, Art. 5.10.11.4.1a

0.01 < ρ = 0.025 < 0.04   OK

A_s = 0.025 × $\pi(48)^2/4$ = 45.24 in^2

Using 29 #11 bars with A_s = 29 × 1.56 = 45.24 in^2 will satisfy the requirement.

(b) Design of spiral reinforcement

Shear stress, Art. 5.8.3

Resistance factor, Art. 1.3.2.1

ϕ = 1.0

where

V_u = 600 kips

B = 48 in.

D_r = 48.0 − 2(2.00 + 0.875) − 1.41 = 40.84 in. (assuming #7 spiral)

$$d_e = \frac{48.0}{2} + \frac{40.84}{\pi} = 37.0 \text{ in.} \qquad \text{Eq. C5.8.2.9-2}$$

d_v = 0.9 d_e = 33.3 in.

Shear carried by concrete, Art. 5.8.3.3

Use β = 2, θ = 45° if $A_{v\,min}$ provided and no tension in column per Art. 5.8.3.4.1

Check if concrete is effective in end regions per Art. 5.10.11.4.1c.

P_u = 2,700 kips

P_u > 0.10(3.5 ksi)(1,810 in^2) = 634 kips   Concrete is effective

$$V_c = 0.0316(2)\sqrt{3.5}(48 \text{ in.})(33.3 \text{ in}) = 189 \text{ kips} \qquad \text{Eq. 5.8.3.3-3}$$

901. **(Continued)**

Spacing of spiral reinforcement, Eq. C5.8.3.3-1

$$s = \text{pitch} = A_v f_y d_v / V_s$$

where

A_v = 0.6 in^2 (Try #7 spiral)
f_y = 60 ksi
b_v = 48 in.
d_v = 33.3 in.

$$V_{s \text{ required}} = \frac{600 - 189(1.0)}{1.0} = 411 \text{ kips}$$

and

$$s = \frac{(2 \times 0.6) \times 60 \times 33.3}{411} = 5.83 \text{ in.} \qquad \text{Use 5.0 in.}$$

Check minimum transverse reinforcing, Art. 5.8.2.5

$$A_{v \text{ min}} \geq 0.0316 \sqrt{f'_c} \, \frac{b_v s}{f_y} = 0.0316\sqrt{3.5} \, \frac{48.0(5.0)}{60} = 0.24 \text{ in}^2 \qquad \text{OK}$$

$$V_s = \frac{A_v f_y d_v}{5} = \frac{(2)(0.60)(60)(33.3)}{5.0} = 480 \text{ kips}$$

The nominal shear resistance V_n is the lesser of:

$$V_n = V_c + V_s = 189 + 480 = 669 \text{ kips} \qquad \text{Governs, OK} \qquad\qquad \text{Eq. 5.8.3.3-1}$$
$$V_n = 0.25 \, f'_c b_v d_v = 0.25(3.5)(48.0)(33.3) = 1,399 \text{ kips} \qquad\qquad \text{Eq. 5.8.3.3-2}$$

Check maximum spacing, Art. 5.10.6.2

$6 \, d_b = 6(1.41) = 8.46$ in.

6 in. governs, 5.0 in. OK

End regions, Art. 5.10.11.4.1c

H_e = length of end region
= column dimension = 48 in.
or = $20 \times 12/6$ = 40 in.
or = 18 in.

Length of the end region = 48 in. Governs

Check confinement, Art. 5.10.11.4.1d

$$\rho_s = 0.45(A_g/A_c - 1)f'_c/f_{yh} = 0.45\left[(1,810/1,521) - 1\right]3.5/60 = 0.0050 \qquad\qquad \text{Eq. 5.7.4.6-1}$$

$$\text{or } \rho_s = 0.12 \, f'_c/f_y = 0.12 \times 3.5/60 = 0.007 \text{ whichever is larger} \qquad\qquad \text{Eq. 5.10.11.4.1d-1}$$

$$\rho_s = 4A_s(\pi D_c) / s\pi D_c^2 = 4A_s/sD_c$$

$$s \leq \frac{4A_s}{\rho_s D_c} = \frac{4(0.6 \text{ in}^2)}{0.007(44 \text{ in.})} = 7.8 \text{ in.}$$

901. (Continued)

Maximum spacing of confinement reinforcement, Art. 5.10.11.4.1e

Maximum spacing of confinement reinforcement is as follows:
    4 in. < 7.8 in. < (48/4 = 12 in.) Use 4 in.

Confinement reinforcement must extend into the cap and
foundation 48/2 = 24 in., but not less than 15 in.   Art. 5.10.11.4.3

(c) Sketch of vertical and spiral reinforcement

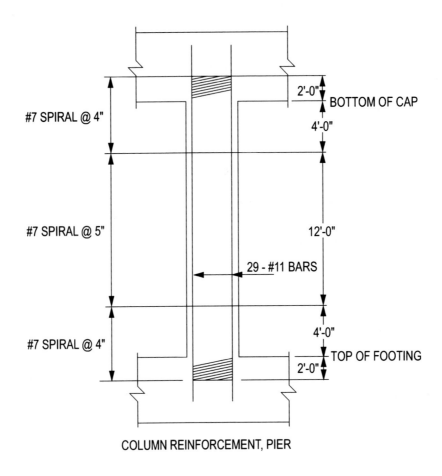

COLUMN REINFORCEMENT, PIER

902. **Determine longitudinal dimension of footing.**

Design for $M_u = 4,900$ ft-kips, $V_u = 650$ kips, $P_u = 3,000$ kips

$\phi_{bcol} = 0.9$ Art. 1.3.2.1 and 5.10.11.4.1b

$$M_{n_{req.}} = \frac{4,900}{(3.0)(0.9)} = 1,815 \text{ ft-kips}$$

$$P_{n_{req.}} = \frac{3,000}{0.9} = 3,333 \text{ kips}$$

$$A_s = 29 \times 1.56 = 45.24 \text{ in}^2$$

$$\rho = \frac{45.24}{\pi(48^2)/4} = 0.025$$

From chart in **Figure 902 B.**

$$M_{n(prov.)} = 4,500 \text{ ft-kips}$$

(Art. 3.10.9.4.1) Foundation factors shall be designed to the lesser of Art. 3.10.9.4.2 or Art. 3.10.9.4.3.

$$\frac{M_u}{(R = 1.0)} = 4,900 \text{ ft-kips}$$ Art. 3.10.9.4.2

$$1.3 \, M_n = 5,850 \text{ ft-kips}$$ Art. 3.10.9.4.3

Design footing for $M_u = 4,900$ ft-kips

Assumption to ignore shear from column in footing design. Actual design would amplify the moment by the column shear (respective to the moment used) by the footing thickness.

$$e_L = \frac{4,900}{3,000} = 1.63 \text{ ft}$$

According to Art. 10.6.4.2 and Art. 11.6.5, the resultant has to be within the middle 2/3 of the footing length.

$$e \leq \left(\frac{L}{2} - \frac{1}{6}L\right) \text{ where } e \leq \frac{3L}{3 \times 2} - \frac{L}{6} = \frac{2L}{6}$$

Therefore, minimum footing dimension in longitudinal direction is:

$$L_{min} = \frac{6e}{2} = \frac{6(1.63)}{2} = 4.89' \approx 4.9'$$

902. **(a) (Continued)**

Nominal bearing capacity = 35 ksf
$\phi_b = 1.0$ for extreme limit state   Art. 10.5.5.3.5 and Art. 11.6.5

The bearing pressure of a footing on rock shall be calculated using a linear distributed pressure, per Art. 11.6.3.2

$$\sigma_{max} = \frac{\Sigma V}{BL}\left(1 + 6\frac{e}{L}\right)$$

$$\sigma_{min} = \frac{\Sigma V}{BL}\left(1 - 6\frac{e}{L}\right)$$

Assuming e_L is within the middle third of footing

$$\frac{(L/3)}{2} \geq e_L = 1.63$$

$$L \geq (1.63)(2)(3) = 9.78 \text{ in.}$$

Try L = 15 ft

$$\sigma_{max} = \frac{3,000}{(15)(10)}\left[1 + 6\left(\frac{1.63}{15}\right)\right] = 33.04 \text{ ksf}$$

$$\phi_b\sigma_{max} = 33 \text{ ksf} < \sigma_{all} = 35 \text{ ksf} \qquad \text{OK}$$

$$\sigma_{min} = \frac{3,000}{(15)(10)}\left[1 - 6\left(\frac{1.63}{15}\right)\right] = 6.96 \text{ ksf}$$

Use 15'-0"-long footing

(b) Determine footing depth and bottom longitudinal reinforcement.

Determine equivalent square column width: Art. 5.13.3.4

$$\sqrt{\pi (r_{col})^2} = \sqrt{\pi (24)^2} \approx 42.54 \text{ in.}$$

$$B_{effect} = 42.54 \text{ in.}$$

Assume footing depth = 3.5 ft.

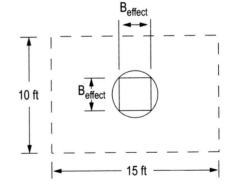

902. (Continued)

Cover (bottom of footing) = 3 in.
  (cast against earth)

Table 5.12.3-1

$$d_{e_L} = 42 \text{ in.} - 3 \text{ in.} - \frac{1.27 \text{ in.}}{2} = 38.37 \text{ in.}$$

$$d_{v_L} = \max(0.9\, d_e, 0.72\, h) = 34.53 \text{ in.}$$ Art. 5.8.2.9

$$d_{e_T} = d_{e_L} - 1.27 \text{ in.} = 37.1 \text{ in.}$$

$$d_{v_T} = \max(0.9\, d_e, 0.72\, h) = 33.39 \text{ in.}$$ Art. 5.8.2.9

Critical face of moment in longitudinal direction: $\frac{15 \text{ ft}}{2} - \frac{42.54 \text{ in.}}{(12 \text{ in./ft})(2)} = 5.73 \text{ ft}$

One-way action

Critical face for shear in both directions:

Longitudinal $\frac{15 \text{ ft}}{2} - \frac{42.54 \text{ in.}}{(12 \text{ in./ft})(2)} - d_{v_L}/12 = 2.85 \text{ ft}$

Transverse $\frac{10 \text{ ft}}{2} - \frac{42.54 \text{ in.}}{(12 \text{ in./ft})(2)} - d_{v_T}/12 = 0.45 \text{ ft}$

Two-way shear critical face is a diameter $= \text{col } \phi + d_v(\text{avg}) = 4 \text{ ft} + \frac{(34.53 + 33.39)}{12 \times 2} = 6.83 \text{ ft}$

Demand on footing

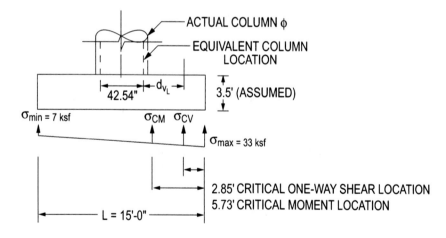

902. (Continued)

Ignoring the weight of footing (assumption)

$\sigma_{CM} = \dfrac{33-7}{15}(15-5.73)+7 = 23.07 \text{ ksf}$ footing pressure at critical moment location

$\sigma_{CV} = \dfrac{33-7}{15}(15-2.85)+7 = 28.06 \text{ ksf}$ footing pressure at critical one-way shear location

$V_{u\,ft} = 28.06(2.85)+\left(\dfrac{33-28.06}{2}\right)(2.85) = 87.02 \text{ kips/ft}$

$M_{u\,ft} = 23.07(5.73)^2\left(\dfrac{1}{2}\right)+\left(\dfrac{33-23.07}{2}\right)(5.73)^2\left(\dfrac{2}{3}\right) = 487.41 \text{ ft-kips/ft}$

Check shear capacity:

One way longitudinal shear capacity   Art. 5.8.3.3

$V_n \le V_c = 0.0316\,\beta\sqrt{f'_c}\,b_v d_{v_L} = 0.0316(2.0)\sqrt{4}\,(12 \text{ in./ft})(34.53) = 52.37 \text{ kips/ft}$ Controls

$\beta = 2.0$ Art. 5.8.3.4.1

$V_n \le 0.25\, f'_c\, b_v d_{v_L} = 0.25(4)(12 \text{ in./ft})(34.53) = 414.34 \text{ kips/ft}$

$\phi_V = 1.0$ (extreme load case)   Art. 1.3.2.1

$\phi_V V_n = 52.37 \text{ kips/ft} < V_{u\,ft} = 87.02 \text{ kips/ft}$ NG

By observation, this is not very close, try 4'-6" footing.

$d_v = \max\,(0.9\,d_e,\, 0.72\,h)$ Art. 5.8.2.9

$d_{e_L} = 38.37 + 12 = 50.37 \text{ in.}$ $d_{v_L} = 45.33 \text{ in.}$

$d_{e_T} = 37.1 + 12 = 49.1 \text{ in.}$ $d_{v_T} = 44.19 \text{ in.}$

Critical face for one-way shear:

Longitudinal $\dfrac{15}{2} - \dfrac{42.54}{(12)(2)} - \dfrac{45.33}{12} = 1.95 \text{ ft}$

Transverse $\dfrac{10}{2} - \dfrac{42.54}{(12)(2)} - \dfrac{44.19}{12} = -0.45 \text{ ft} < 0$

Two-way shear critical face

$4 \text{ ft} + \dfrac{45.33 + 44.19}{(12)(2)} = 7.73 \text{ ft} < 10 \text{ ft}$

$\sigma_{CV} = \dfrac{33-7}{15}(15-1.95)+7 = 29.62 \text{ ksf}$ (footing pressure at critical one-way shear location)

$V_{ult} = 29.62(1.95) + \dfrac{33-29.62}{2}(1.95) = 61.06 \text{ kips/ft}$

$V_n \le 0.0316(2)\sqrt{4}\,(12 \text{ in./ft})(45.33) = 68.75 \text{ kips/ft}$

$\phi_V V_n = 1.0(68.75) = 68.75 \text{ kips/ft} > 61.06 \text{ kips/ft}$ OK

902. (Continued)

Check two-way shear:

$$V_n = \left(0.063 + \frac{0.126}{\beta_c}\right)\sqrt{f_c'}\, b_o d_v \leq 0.126\sqrt{f_c'}\, b_o d_v \qquad \text{Art. 5.13.3.6.3-1}$$

$$d_{v_{avg}} = \frac{45.36 + 44.19}{2} = 44.76 \text{ in.}$$

$$b_o = \pi D = \pi(7.73)(12 \text{ in./ft}) = 291.41 \text{ in.}$$

$$\beta_c = 1.0 \quad \text{circular}$$

$$V_n = \left(0.063 + \frac{0.126}{1.0}\right)\sqrt{4}\,(291.41)(44.76) = 4,930 \text{ kips}$$

$$V_n = 0.126\sqrt{4}\,(291.41)(44.76) = 3,287 \text{ kips} \qquad \text{Controls}$$

$$\sigma_{avg} = \left(\frac{33 + 7}{2}\right) = 20 \text{ ksf} \qquad \text{average stress under column}$$

$$V_u = 3,000 - \left[\frac{\pi(7.73)^2}{4}(20)\right] = 2,061 \text{ kips}$$

$$\phi_v V_n = 1.0(3,287) = 3,287 \text{ kips} > V_u = 2,061 \text{ kips} \qquad \text{OK}$$

Use a 4'-6" thick footing

Determine the number of longitudinal bars required at base of footing. Note that there is no uplift on footing, so top mat would meet minimum requirements in the code.
$$M_{u\,ft} = 487.41 \text{ ft-kips/ft } (12) = 5,849 \text{ in.-kips/ft}$$

Maximum reinforcement limits deleted in 2005 interim

Minimum reinforcement $\qquad\qquad\qquad\qquad\qquad\qquad\qquad\qquad$ Art. 5.7.3.3.2

$$M_{cr} = \gamma_3\left[(\gamma_1 f_r + \gamma_2 f_{epe})S_c - M_{dnc}\left(\frac{S_c}{S_{nc}} - 1\right)\right]$$

$$f_r = 0.24\sqrt{f_c'} = 0.48 \text{ ksi} \qquad\qquad \gamma_1 = 1.6 \qquad \gamma_3 = 0.75 \qquad \text{Art. 5.4.2.6}$$

$$M_{cr} = 0.75\left[(1.6 \times 0.48 \text{ ksi} + \gamma_2 \times 0)\left(\frac{12 \times (4.5 \times 12)^2}{6}\right) - 0\right] = 3,359 \text{ in.-kips/ft}$$

$$\text{Min } (M_{cr}/1.33\, M_u) = \min(3,359/7,779) = 3,359 \text{ in.-kips/ft} < M_{u\,ft} = 5,849 \text{ in.-kips/ft}$$

$$M_u = 5,849 \text{ in.-kips/ft}$$

$$a = \frac{A_s f_y}{0.85\, f_c'\, b_w} \qquad\qquad\qquad\qquad\qquad\qquad\qquad\qquad \text{Art. 5.7.3.1.2-4}$$

$$M_n = A_s f_y\left(d - \frac{a}{2}\right) \qquad\qquad\qquad\qquad\qquad\qquad\qquad \text{Art. 5.7.3.2.2-1}$$

Note: control of cracking by distribution of flexural reinforcement in Art. 5.7.3.4 is determined at the service load case, so it is not performed in this problem.

902. (Continued)

$(10 \text{ ft})(12) - 2(3\text{-in. cover} + 1.27/2 \text{ in.}) = 112.73 \text{ in.}$

M_n (total footing) use M_u

$\qquad = 5,849 \text{ in.-kips/ft} \times 12 \text{ ft} = 70,188 \text{ in.-kips}$

$d = 4.5 \text{ ft} \times 12 = 54 \text{ in.} - 3 \text{ in. (cover)} - \dfrac{1.27}{2} = 50.37 \text{ in.}$

Assume $a = 3.0 \text{ in.}$

$A_s = \dfrac{70,188}{60 \times (50.37 - 3/2)} = 23.94 \text{ in}^2$

No. #10 bars $= \dfrac{23.94}{1.27} = 18.85$

Use 19 # 10 bars

Check a

$a = \dfrac{A_s f_y}{0.85 \, bf'_c} = \dfrac{(19 \times 1.27)(60)}{0.85(12 \times 12)(4)} = 2.96 \text{ in.} < 3.0 \text{ in., assumed}$

$M_n = (19 \times 1.27)(60)\left(50.37 - \dfrac{2.96}{2}\right) = 70,783 \text{ in.-kips} > 70,188$

Bar spacing $= 114.73 \text{ in.}/(18 \text{ spaces}) = 6.4 \text{ in.}$

$\phi_b = 1.0$ Art. 1.3.2.1

$\phi_b M_n = 5,899 \text{ in.-kips/ft} > M_u = 5,849 \text{ in.-kips/ft} \qquad$ OK

903. Introduction

Given:
$$PGA = 0.55$$
$$S_S = 1.40$$
$$S_1 = 0.58$$

Since the soil profile is hard rock, according to Table 3.10.3.1-1 the site class shall be A.

According to Article 3.10.3.2, the site factors shall be:

$F_{pga} = 0.8$ Table 3.10.3.2-1

$F_a = 0.8$ Table 3.10.3.2-2

$F_V = 0.8$ Table 3.10.3.2-3

$\therefore A_S = F_{pga} \, PGA = 0.8 \times 0.55 = 0.44$ Art.3.10.4.2

$S_{DS} = F_a S_s = 0.8 \times 1.40 = 1.12$

$S_{D1} = F_v S_1 = 0.8 \times 0.58 = 0.46$

$0.3 < S_{D1} \leq 0.5$ $\therefore$ Zone 3   Table 3.10.6.1

$T_S = \dfrac{S_{D1}}{S_{DS}} = \dfrac{0.46}{1.12} = 0.41 \sec$

$T_o = 0.2 T_S = 0.2 \times 0.41 = 0.082 \sec$

Since the bridge is considered regular (Table 4.7.4.3.1-2) and is a multispan classified as "Other," the Uniform Load Elastic Method or the Single-Mode Elastic Method can be used per Table 4.7.4.3.1-1(both methods are given here but only one method is required to be used). According to Article 3.10.8, the seismic forces shall be determined in two orthogonal directions along the centerline of the bridge.

The weights of the superstructure to be calculated include those of the box girder, the added part of the diaphragms over the pier caps, the parapets, and half the weight of the columns. The average weight per linear foot is calculated as shown below.

w_d = weight of hollow deck, given	=	8.77 klf
w_c = added weight of the diaphragms over the pier caps		
$\quad = 3$ piers $\times 4$ cells $\times (6 \times 4.42' \times 6.25' \times 0.150)/206$	=	1.45 klf
w_p = weight of two parapets $= 2 \times 0.420$, given	=	0.84 klf
w_{c1} = half the weight of the four columns of Piers 1 and 3		
$\quad = 4[\pi(1.5)^2 \times 10 \times 0.15]/206 = 42.40/206$	=	0.21 klf
w_{c2} = half the weight of the two columns of Pier 2		
$\quad = 2[\pi(2.0)^2 \times 10 \times 0.15]/206 = 37.70/206$	=	0.18 klf
Average weight	=	11.45 klf

903. (Continued)

Procedure 1 – Uniform Load Method, Longitudinal Force   Art. 4.7.4.3.2c

$$T_m = 2\pi\sqrt{\frac{W}{gK}}$$ Eq. C4.7.4.3.2c-3

Calculation of the seismic forces in the longitudinal direction is as follows:

K = total stiffness of all columns of Piers 1, 2, and 3

K = four columns of Piers 1 and 3 and two columns of Pier 2

$$K_{total} = 4 \times 12 \frac{EI_1}{h^3} + 2 \times 12 \frac{EI_2}{h^3}$$

E = 3,403 ksi   given

h = 20 ft

W = 11.45 klf × 206 ft = 2,360 kips

$$I_1 \text{ (Piers 1 and 3)} = \frac{\pi d^4}{64} = \frac{\pi (3^4)}{64} = 3.98 \text{ ft}^4 \text{ (one column)}$$

$$I_2 \text{ (Pier 2)} = \frac{\pi d^4}{64} = \frac{\pi (4^4)}{64} = 12.57 \text{ ft}^4 \text{ (one column)}$$

$$K_{pier\,1} + K_{pier\,3} = 4 \text{ columns} \times 12 \times 490,000 \times 3.98/20^3 = 11,700 \text{ kips/ft}$$

$$K_{pier\,2} = 2 \text{ columns} \times 12 \times 490,000 \times 12.58/20^3 = 18,500 \text{ kips/ft}$$

$$K_{total} = \overline{\overline{30,200 \text{ kips/ft}}}$$

g = acceleration of gravity = 32.2 ft/sec²

$$T_m = 2\pi\sqrt{\frac{2,360}{32.2 \times 30,200}} = 0.31 \text{ sec}$$

$T_o < T_m < T_s$

$C_{sm} = S_{DS}$ Eq. 3.10.4.2-4

$C_{sm} = 1.12$

p_e = Total equivalent static earthquake loading = $C_{sm}W = 1.12 \times 2,360 = 2,640$ kips

$$V_{L,\,pier\,2} = p_e \times \frac{K_{pier\,2}}{\Sigma_{total}} = 2,640 \times \left(\frac{18,500}{30,200}\right) = 1,620 \text{ kips}$$

$$M_{L,\,pier\,2} = V_{L,\,pier\,2} \times \frac{h}{2} = 1,620 \times \left(\frac{20}{2}\right) = 16,200 \text{ ft-kips}$$

$$= 8,100 \text{ ft-kips/column}$$

Axial forces due to overturning effect from the longitudinal earthquake load are negligible by inspection.

903. (Continued)

Procedure 1 – Uniform Load Method, Transverse Force   Art. 4.7.4.3.2c

Since the stiffness of the bridge is the same in the longitudinal and transverse directions, the seismic load in the transverse direction is also the same. Therefore,

$$V_{T, \text{pier } 2} = 1,620 \text{ kips}$$

Compute the earthquake bending moments and overturning axial forces at the base of Pier 2.

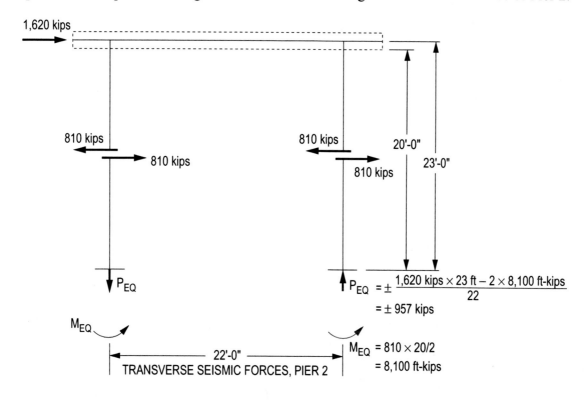

TRANSVERSE SEISMIC FORCES, PIER 2

Procedure 2 – Single-Mode Spectral Method, Longitudinal Force   Art. 4.7.4.3.2b

From the Procedure 1 calculations:

$K_{1,3}$ = 11,700 kips/ft
K_2 = 18,500 kips/ft

$$v_s(x) = \text{horizontal deflection of deck} = \frac{P_o L}{\sum K}$$

$$= \frac{(1 \text{ kip/ft} \times 206 \text{ ft})}{(11,700 + 18,500) \text{ kips/ft}}$$

$$= 0.00682 \text{ ft}$$

903. (Continued)

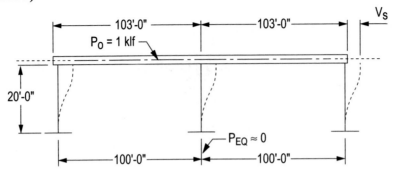

LONGITUDINAL DEFORMATION OF THE BRIDGE

$$T_m = \text{period of vibration} = 2\pi\sqrt{\frac{\gamma}{p_o g \alpha}} \qquad \text{Eq. C4.7.4.3.2b-4}$$

$$p_e(x) = \text{equivalent static earthquake loading} = \frac{\beta C_{sm}}{\gamma} w(x) v_s(x) \qquad \text{Eq. C4.7.4.3.2b-5}$$

$$g = \text{acceleration of gravity} = 32.2 \text{ ft/sec}^2$$

$$\alpha = \int v_s(x)\, dx \qquad \text{Eq. C4.7.4.3.2b-1}$$

$$\beta = \int w(x) v_s(x)\, dx \qquad \text{Eq. C4.7.4.3.2b-2}$$

$$\gamma = \int w(x) v_s^2(x)\, dx \qquad \text{Eq. C4.7.4.3.2b-3}$$

Using the expressions above, the equivalent static force can be calculated as follows:

$$\alpha = \int_0^{206} v_s(x)\,dx = \int_0^{206} 0.00682\, dx$$

$$= 0.00682 \times 206 = 1.41 \text{ ft}^2$$

$$\beta = \int_0^{206} w(x) v_s(x)\, dx = w(x)\int_0^{206} 0.00682\, dx$$

$$= 11.45 \times 1.41 = 16.1 \text{ ft-kips}$$

$$\gamma = \int_0^{206} w(x) v_s^2(x)\, dx$$

$$= 11.45(0.00682)^2 \times 206 = 0.11 \text{ ft}^2\text{-kips}$$

$$T_m = 2\pi\sqrt{\frac{\gamma}{p_o g \alpha}} = 2\pi\sqrt{\frac{0.110}{1.0 \times 32.2 \times 1.41}} = 0.31 \text{ sec} \qquad \text{Eq. C4.7.4.3.2b-4}$$

$$C_{sm} = 1.12 \text{ (As determined in Procedure 1)}$$

$$p_e(x) = \frac{16.1 \times 1.12}{0.11} \times 11.45 \times 0.00682 = 12.8 \text{ kips/ft} \qquad \text{Eq. C4.7.4.3.2b-5}$$

$$p_e = 12.8 \times 206 = 2,640 \text{ kips}$$

903. (Continued)

As can be seen from Procedure 1, both the uniform load and single-mode spectral method will result in the same longitudinal elastic seismic forces at Pier 2 for this structure.

Procedure 2 – Single-Mode Spectral Method, Transverse Force   Art. 4.7.4.3.2b

Given that the hint in the problem requirement indicated that the deflected shape of the superstructure due to a uniform transverse force can be assumed to be a uniform transverse displacement and since the stiffness of the structure is the same in the longitudinal and transverse directions, the transverse period and equivalent static earthquake loading will be the same as that calculated in the longitudinal direction.

The transverse elastic seismic forces at Pier 2 will be the same as those previously calculated using Procedure 1.

Combination of seismic force effects   Art. 3.10.8
Load Case 1 = 100% longitudinal + 30% transverse
Load Case 2 = 30% longitudinal + 100% transverse

Load Cases 1 and 2 for the longitudinal and transverse seismic forces are shown in the following table:

Force	Load Case 1 100% Long F + 30% Trans F			Load Case 2 30% Long F + 100% Trans F		
V_L	$810 + 0$	$=$	810 kips	$0.3(810) + 0$	$=$	243 kips
V_T	$0 + 0.3(810)$	$=$	243 kips	$0 + 810$	$=$	810 kips
P	$0 + 0.3(957)$	$=$	± 287 kips	$0 + 957$	$=$	±957 kips
M_L	$8,100 + 0$	$=$	$8,100$ ft-kips	$0.3(8,100) + 0$	$=$	$2,430$ ft-kips
M_T	$0 + 0.3(8,100)$	$=$	$2,430$ ft-kips	$0 + 8,100$	$=$	$8,100$ ft-kips

According to Table 3.4.1-1 for Extreme Event I:

$1.25DC + 1.0EQ$

The above equation requires combining seismic Load Cases 1 and 2 with the dead load forces as given in the problem statement.

DC = dead load axial force in column of Pier 2 = 664 kips

903. **(Continued)**

According to Table 3.10.7.1-1, Art. 3.10.7.1, the response modification factor R for multiple column bents with an importance category of "Other" is 5. (It is common practice in high-seismic regions to apply the R factor only to moments.) The seismic moments should be divided by R and combined with the dead load moments. The following table shows the modified elastic design moments.

Determine the maximum forces:

Force	Load Case 1 1.25(DC) ± 1.0(EQ)			Load Case 2 1.25(DC) ± 1.0(EQ)		
V_L	1.25(0) + 1.0(810)	=	810 kips	1.25(0) +1.0(243)	=	243 kips
V_T	1.25(21) + 1.0(243)	=	269 kips	1.25(21) + 1.0(810)	=	836 kips
P_{max}	1.25(664) + 1.0(287)	=	1,117 kips	1.25(664) + 1.0(957)	=	1,787 kips
M_L	1.25(0) + 1.0(8,100/5)	=	1,620 ft-kips	1.25(0) + 1.0(2,430/5)	=	486 ft-kips
M_T	1.25(162) + 1.0(2,430/5)	=	689 ft-kips	1.25(162) + 1.0(8,100/5)	=	1,820 ft-kips

The above table indicates that the combination for Load Case 2 governs.

M_u = factored moment = $(486^2 + 1,820^2)^{1/2} = 1,884$ ft-kips

V_u = factored shear = $(243^2 + 836^2)^{1/2} = 871$ kips

The summary of maximum design forces at the base of each column of Pier 2 is as follows:

M_u = 1,884 ft-kips

V_u = 871 kips

P_u = 1,787 kips

PE Practice Exams Published by NCEES

Chemical

Civil: Construction

Civil: Geotechnical

Civil: Structural

Civil: Transportation

Civil: Water Resources and Environmental

Electrical and Computer: Computer Engineering

Electrical and Computer: Electrical and Electronics

Electrical and Computer: Power

Environmental

Mechanical: HVAC and Refrigeration

Mechanical: Mechanical Systems and Materials

Mechanical: Thermal and Fluids Systems

For more information about these and other NCEES publications and services, visit NCEES.org or call Client Services at (800) 250-3196.